A VOICE IN THE FOREST
Spirit Conversations with Alex Sanders King of the Witches

By Jimahl diFiosa

2022 Jimahl diFiosa©
1999 Jimahl diFiosa©
2004 Harvest Shadows Publications©
2022 Published by RedFaun Press©
www.redfaunpress.com

9 781387 709199

All rights reserved. No part of this publication may be reproduced stored in or introduced into a retrieval system, or transmitted, in any form or by any means (electronic, mechanical, photocopying, recording, or otherwise), except in the case of brief quotations embodied in critical articles or reviews, without the prior written permission of both the copyright owner and the above publisher of this book.

RedFaun Press© 2022 Revised Edition

Cover art and book design by Karagan Edited by Karagan Griffith

Cover Photograph by Jimahl diFiosa, 2022

New unpublished Photographs by Karagan Griffith

If this book is sold without a cover, it is stolen property. It was reported as "unsold and destroyed" to the publisher, and neither the author nor the publisher has received any payment for this "stripped book."

A Voice in the Forest

Jimahl DiFiosa

For Finbar, a forever friend and a devoted Priest of the Goddess who met the Ferryman too soon

As She told us so many years ago on that mountain top: "You are the Magic"

A Voice in the Forest

Jimahl DiFiosa

"The woods are lovely, dark and deep. But I have promises to keep, And miles to go before I sleep..."

Robert Frost

A Voice in the Forest

Jimahl DiFiosa

REVIEWS FROM THE FIRST EDITION

from Rosemary Edghill, author of Bell, Book, and Murder
"A VOICE IN THE FOREST is a touching, astounding, and inspiring book. Whether it contains the true last words of Alex Sanders is something that every reader will have to decide for himself, but no matter what decision you come to, this book's powerful wisdom will engage your mind and touch your heart."

from Chas S. Clifton, reviewer
"...A VOICE IN THE FOREST should interest anyone concerned with issues of mediumship and the establishment of what are sometimes called magickal 'contacts' within revived Witchcraft. Modern practitioners do frequently refer to the presence of ancestral spirits and deceased Witches who take an interest in their religious descendants' activities....
...The narrative pace is quick and the description of the coven's necromantic ritual on Hallowe'en 1998—and its unintended consequences for one member— is reminiscent of Dion Fortune's The Secrets of Dr. Taverner, albeit more compressed. Most importantly, it raises a question that many if not most Wiccan groups gloss over: the importance of magickal 'contacts.'
... It takes an author like Jimahl... to remind us that communication with discarnate spiritual ancestors remains important to some modern Witches.... Here is an opportunity for further scholarly investigation...."

from Dianis, Starkindler.org
"I think you will be entranced by this book. Once I'd started reading it, I was unable to put it down until I had turned the last page.
Do I think they really contacted the spirit of Alex Sanders? I will have to leave ... [that] ... to people who knew Alex in the flesh; but I do believe his spirit, and the spirit of his tradition, speak through this book. I was moved to tears many times as I turned its pages. I recommend it heartily to all who wish to touch the mystery that was Alex, and to all who love the goddess and the Craft.
Do read this book; I believe it is an important and inspiring book, and I

believe that if you read it you'll be very glad you did."

Starspawn, Alexandrian Wicca Elder
"I first approached the book with skepticism as I heard it was channeled through a '[spirit]' board, but since it was written by an old friend, I read it.
I was amazed at what I found. From the first moment I opened the book, it had me mesmerized. I never personally met Alex Sanders, but his life and legacy touched every part of my being, from my religious awakening, to the shaping of my morality, to the crafting of spells and potions, to the way I looked upon the world and wanted the world to look upon my work.

The book held all I hold sacred in the image of my teacher. At moments, I laughed with its humor and felt tears splash my face with its quiet inspiration and endearing images. Here was my teacher, Alex, as I found him in my dreams as a kind, loving father, brother, friend to the Craft and to me, myself. This book radiated all these emotions and its words will remain with me as I live out the rest of my life. Thank you for bringing this man back into my life!"

from 'Horns and Crescent,' reviewed by Lauren
"[A VOICE IN THE FOREST]... evolves into a spiritual quest, so to speak, by one member of the group to determine exactly what Sanders is up to on the astral....

If contact with Sanders had been limited to the spirit board, I would probably remain skeptical.... But the means of contact escalates from sessions with the board to necromancy and beyond. Sanders is literally stuck between the worlds, hovering over his 'family,' looking for a way to re-enter the earthly plane to impart his messages. He finds a ready and willing vessel in Jimahl.
But this book is about a lot more than that. It follows Jimahl's innermost thoughts through the wheel of his year and his journey of self discovery.

People of all religions, at one time or another, experience crises of faith, the proverbial 'dark night of the soul.' Jimahl hints at major problems afflicting his Wiccan family, but ultimately his communications with Alex strengthen and renew his own ties to the Craft.

Whether you believe this tale or not, Jimahl has written a beautiful and concise book that is hard to put down. I highly recommend it – and leave you with Sander's words: 'And so the Craft goes on – it never dies. It never stops. It can't – you must see to that. I could care less if you use my name 100 years from now. But the goddess must have her due worship.'"

from Christopher Penczak, 'The Second Road'
"A VOICE IN THE FOREST is a very unusual read. In fact, I must say I've never read a book like it. Subtitled 'A Conversation with Alex Sanders,' the premise of the book is that a group of Alexandrian Witches contact the spirit of Alex Sanders, founder of Alexandrian Witchcraft and often called 'King of Witches,' ten years after his death. The book is part narrative of the author's experience and part transcript of these spirit board and channeling sessions.
Not being a big fan of traditions named after and reverent to a single person, wasn't sure how I would respond to this book, but I feel it has words for not only those of the Alexandrian tradition, but most neo-pagan groups.

... the sense of genuine honesty is pervasive throughout the book. Even if you don't believe that Jimahl contacted Sanders, you finish the book feeling he truly believes he did. And after some thought, I'm inclined to agree, but the source of the message is not as important as the message itself. Alex Sanders gives the witchcraft community ... the message of true magic along with responsibility, goddess reverence, education and preserving the Craft. They are all thoughts to keep in the forefront of our minds as we head into the new aeon."

from Mike Gleason, reviewer
"This is a book that can be, and probably will be, read in one sitting. It is

clearly written and not at all difficult to understand.... It is composed of information which Alex Sanders wanted to share with his Craft children and the other Hidden Children of the Goddess.
It is very difficult for me to be objective about this book. It is about the founder of my particular path, written by an individual who shares that path with me ... I must say that, honestly, it rings true
for me.

I emailed Jimahl just before I started reading... this book to relate one small thing which convinces me of the validity of his communication. Many years ago (in the early 1970s) I received a pack of photocopied lecture notes from Alex to aid me in my studies. These notes were later edited to become 'The Alex Sanders Lectures.' The thrill that went through me, and which sent a chill down my spine, as I started to read this book matched the thrill I had when I began reading those notes. It is not a feeling that I have had often in my life."

from 'The Guardian,' the Alexandrian Newsletter; reviewed by Chyrea
"This is a heartfelt and earnest accounting of a significant occurrence for Jimahl. No spirit contact should be taken lightly. There are important messages from those who have passed before that can aid us in the mortal presence. I found it to be moving and engrossing, and invite all to share his phenomenal experience. Blessed Be."

from "The Silver Circle," reviewed by Merlin
"This is a book like no other, and actually it contains two stories. On the one hand it is a rare account of how a coven works together, how magic and dreams and rituals all gravitate towards a common purpose. On the other hand it is the story of how a coven contacted the spirit of Alex Sanders, and the messages that came through.

... This (book) gives us a fascinating insight into how a coven works, what its people experience, and also what can go wrong.... as an intimate insight into the workings of a coven, this book is definitely worth buying!"

Jimahl DiFiosa

from "The Crow's Calling," reviewed by Deb Jarvis
"I walked around for a few weeks trying to figure out exactly what it was about the book that made it ring so true. I would have days where I would almost get it, and then I'd find myself with the book in hand again, reexamining a salient point or poignant phrase. I concluded after a long soul search that it was the honesty in which
the channeled messages were given, both by 'the spirit' and by Jimahl.
... The fact that he followed his vision, he followed his truth, gave it the solidity and the validity that made me, the skeptic who needs proof and does not just accept things at face value, believe.

This book contains a message that we all need to hear, especially in these days of confusion and conflict. If we are to fulfill this vision, and become an accepted religious group, beyond persecution and prejudice, we should take these messages and pass them on. They have weight and merit. They are things that we all need to hear. Read it, take a moment to still the inner chaos, and listen..."

A Voice in the Forest

ACKNOWLEDGMENTS

This book could never have been completed without the limitless encouragement of the following people:

Morven, my teacher and friend, who is always ready with a word of encouragement when I need it most.

Paul, Phoenix, Asha, and Finbar — for your unwavering faith in the finished project.

Loriel — I am so grateful to Alex for bringing us together.

And to everyone involved in these remarkable events — this is not only a story about Alex — it is also a story about each of us.

Thank you all so very much.

Jimahl
October 25, 2003

A Voice in the Forest

Jimahl DiFiosa

CONTENTS

Prologue to this new edition **21**

Foreword **27**

Preface **33**

Introduction **37**

A Voice in the Forest **41**

Necromancy **61**

The Second Group Session **77**

Dreams and Questions **93**

Descent into Winter **101**

A Light in the Forest **109**

Asha and Finbar Meet Alex **119**

Promises to Keep **131**

Asha and Jimahl Contact Alex **143**

Dark Water **151**

Photographs **167**

The Final Communication **173**

The Green that Keeps on Growing **179**

Afterthoughts **187**

Epilogue 1999 **195**

Lammas Session 2002 **201**

Lammas Session 2003 **219**

Epilogue for the Second Edition **237**

Unedited Channeling Sessions **247**

Alex Sanders on Adeptness **257**

Responses **269**

Jimahl DiFiosa

A Voice in the Forest

Jimahl DiFiosa

PROLOGUE TO THIS NEW EDITION

I wrote the final words of "A Voice in the Forest" in 1998 as I sat on a deck overlooking the ocean on Cape Cod Bay, MA. It was a hot June day and I was glad to be out of the sun. The tide had gone out as I worked on the last chapter, but was now returning. Gentle swells of water lapped at the wooden pilings beneath me. It seems a life time ago now.

I was sure at the time that I had reached the end of a long journey.
"Be strong in purpose and pure in heart. As long as a circle is cast, as long as the name of the goddess is invoked, she will manifest and grow fat with worship. I cannot say more than that. Never quit. Never stop, for the effort alone carries you forward."

In 2004 I was asked to write a few more words for a new edition of the book. Several new chapters were subsequently born, which chronicled further communication with the spirit of Alex Sanders. Far from being silent, Alex's "voice" had continued to speak in profound ways. There was a renewed urgency to his messages. His words were not about surrender, but about perseverance.
"We must continue to probe the dark for answers. If we fail to do this, we assimilate the mistakes of the past and our condition becomes hopeless. For what is stagnant is spoiled. What is inert has no life. What has no life is dead. The secret is that there is never a need to be dead."

I remember sending the new chapters off to the publisher with the secret hope that my latest efforts would truly be the end of it. While pleased to know that "Voice: continued to delight and inspire readers, I personally found the experience of constantly communicating with the dead (Alex or otherwise) exhausting. As anyone prone to mediumship can attest, it is often difficult to function in the physical world when one foot is planted firmly in the other. I often found myself wishing that Alex would finally move on – in whatever way that was supposed to happen – and leave me in peace.

Perhaps in answer to my inner desires, it was quiet for a few years. Once in a while a friend, or stranger, would show up at the door and ask to speak with Alex. I usually refused (as politely as possible of course), but once in a while, if I sensed a real need, I would try my best to accommodate – often with mixed results.

A particular passage from the narrative of the Lammas 2003 Alex communication (included in this edition) concerning the Greek legend of Charon, the Ferryman of the Dead, preoccupied my thoughts. My theory was that metaphorically Alex needed someone to pay his fare across the Styx before he could move on. I found a further reference to what I assumed was the Ferryman in transcripts of that particular Ouija session. Alex asked for a "coin memorial."

In 2010 I finally acted on my hunch that the "coin memorial" was not an actual financial arrangement, but a type of written tribute to Alex. I was subsequently inspired to write a new biography of the man entitled "A Coin for the Ferryman, the Death and Life of Alex Sanders." In this book I tried, as much as possible, to tell the true story of the man – good, bad and indifferent – or as some of his closest friends referred to him - "a saint and a demon – often at the same time." I was hopeful that these final efforts would forever exorcize the restless spirit that continued to haunt the corridors of my mind. I may have been onto something because shortly after publication of the biography, I had a most amazing dream.

I was walking at night in a strange city by the sea. I could smell the salt in the air. Fog drifted in from the open water and wrapped the landscape in a thick, damp blanket. I crossed a bridge, went down some creaky wooden stairs that led to the water's edge, and found myself standing in front of a pub which sat at the end of a long wooden pier. The place looked deserted but the door was open so I went inside. The long narrow room was nearly empty except for a barkeep, busy tidying up, and a lone patron who sat at the far end of the pub next to an open fire. As I walked toward the figure, I recognized him to be Alex Sanders.

"I've been waiting for you" he said, rising for a second to offer me his hand.
I sat down across from him and we stared at each other. The light from the fire slowly warmed me and brought a bit of added cheer to the darkened room.

The barkeep brought a mug of hot tea – no doubt fortified by whatever earthly spirits were available at that late hour – and we talked quietly for what seemed like hours. I remember his bright eyes, his pale hands and his laughter. We spoke about the most profound things, I'm sure of it. Although afterward I couldn't remember a thing.

"The sacrifice of memory is a necessary exchange for spending time in the land of the dead" Alex explained, "there are things here you may not know of, and still live."

There was a large ship moored at the end of the pier. I had a sense that all of Alex's possessions were safely stowed aboard. I had imagined a smaller vessel, a rowboat perhaps. Alex, as if reading my thoughts, smiled and said "The King of the Witches requires a bigger boat."

He took up a few coins from the table, change that was left by the barkeep after paying our bill, and stood up.
"It's time" was all he said. "Thank you."

And then he was gone.

As I write once again what I hope to be the final "final" words of "A Voice in the Forest" I think not of Alex, but the legacy that he has left behind. It's no longer just about him, not that it ever was, much to the disappointment of his naysayers.

A Voice in the Forest

For 34 years after his death, the Alexandrian tradition of witchcraft is stronger than ever. Men and women continue to arrive on this path from all over the world. They come from the most unlikely places. Some of them write to tell me that they were first inspired to the Craft by my book. I am humbled by this, but then I realized long ago that "A Voice in the Forest" was never about me.

It is, instead, a simple story of one man who refused to be silenced by death. It is a story without an ending for "as long as the heart of the Craft beats fiercely, the book of our lives can never truly be finished."

Today, as I write these words, I find notes from what I believe to have been the last Ouija session with Alex dated 2009, tucked away in an old journal.

During that session, Alex predicted "a renaissance of power that will change
all that it touches." At the time, the phrase made no sense, and little thought was given as to its meaning.
But in retrospect that's exactly what happened and continues to happen. Despite all adversity, both from inside and outside the Craft, the power finds its way.

Perhaps the story is not over, after all.

Jimahl DiFiosa

A Voice in the Forest

Jimahl DiFiosa

FOREWORD
An invocation of Alex Sanders

Alex, the last time I saw you was on the beach at Bexhill. We were collecting driftwood for the fire up at Chantry Cottage and you walked alone, a small figure lost in the folds of an orange parka. It was windy, with the tide out and men with lamps digging for lugworm along the sands; a yellow-green day, the sort of day for an apocalypse. The things you said seemed to take their meaning from the sea and sky. You were low, said your life had been a series of disasters. I was dismayed. One expects magickians to triumph. Looking for driftwood, we talked of drifting. "Look at me," you said, "doing nothing, living nothing, being nothing. Waiting in the womb of the world – stuck." You turned to me with a sad smile and asked, "How can you write about things like that?"
I was to be your biographer. No, not another catalogue of gimcrack wonders, but the real warts-and-all story of your life. If, as many claimed, you were a charlatan, that was okay, too. In fact, that made it more interesting. You were all for telling the seamier side. Telling about going on stage with 'Black Widow' and evoking Astaroth using – as the lead singer disingenuously boasted – "the right chants and everything." Or the time you did a fire ritual in Selmeston village hall wearing a gold lamé g-string and singed your pubic hair. You loved to shock. Do you remember travelling on the London tube with your witches – Rusty, Charles, thrice- witchy
Wendy – all wearing ceremonial robes? We were going to the British Museum to look at the mummies and have a lesson in Egyptian magick. How you talked, talked, talked, how apt was your witch name, Verbius. You drew a crowd and made a most convincing magus, but I don't believe you ever quite convinced yourself.
I said, "I'll write as I find." You agreed. But every time I came to visit I'd find you busy, or tired, or facetious, or in any event soon saying, "Fuck this, Lor, let's go for a pint." And that's what we did, with rain pattering on

the grimy windows of the de la Warr pavilion, on that last day. A woman who had come with me was demanding reassurances about her love life and you gazed at her through a lump of green glass you'd found on the beach. Afterwards she said you'd been scrying the angels warring in her soul, and never understood why I laughed.

In the chapel at your funeral, a witch played guitar and sang. Afterwards, we piled out into the May sunshine. There were people I hadn't seen for years. It turned into a big party. The following weekend "The News Of The World" ran a picture of us, me among the rest, under the banner: THE TWO HUNDRED WICKEDEST PEOPLE IN BRITAIN.

Your friend 'J' was there, hiding from the cameras. He had found the horns that crowned you 'King of the Witches.' You once told me he was the most powerful magician in England. I was alarmed when you introduced us, but he became like a father to me and I have you to thank for our twenty-five year friendship. Around J, stuff happened that defied the imagination. He said you had shown him things more magickal yet, "Alex is a very mysterious man." J was a mystic with his feet firmly on the earth. In one of his poems he wrote, "A child calls, the myriad things are wondrously ordinary." He was as secretive as you were flamboyant, but he had the highest regard for you. Others saw robes, J saw the inner man. You didn't clown about with him. He was one of the few you allowed into that dark chamber of the soul where you spent so much time alone. Alex, do you remember the night of my initiation in the basement at Notting Hill? I had forgotten to bring a black-handled knife and you gave me one of yours (which to this day lives in my sock drawer, its blade tarnished from disuse). There was a journalist present. He'd never seen a witch ritual before. Who would guess that he would be inspired enough to ask for initiation himself, and go on to write books that fired the imaginations of who-knows-how- many thousands of others? I was in touch with Stewart before his death. "Wouldn't Alex be amazed," I emailed him at his home in Ireland, "if he could just see what he started?"

Alex, from your vantage point in the realms of the dread lords of the outer spaces, I do hope you realise what you've done. If it hadn't been for your prodigious oat-sowing, your wholesale initiation of hundreds of unsuitables like me, how would the suburban-kitchen witchcraft of Gardner ever have turned into the World Wide Wicca? Would there be thousands of pagan groups all over the world, entire lineages proudly claiming you as an ancestor? Would the worship of the goddess be reviving in, of all places, the Internet?

'Congratulations Witches!!! Due to the hard work by Texas Pagan Awareness Online and just plain tenacity of the Pagan community, CyberPatrol has said "YES" to Pagan sites.
Bizarre! When you came here to Sussex, you talked of making a haven where witches could escape prejudice. Could you guess that it would one day come into being, not in this most magical of English counties, but in the sacred sites of cyberspace? If I'd really been prescient and, like our colleague Old Mother Shipton, had seen the future, would you have believed me? I can just imagine you in the pub, laughing, winking and saying "Hark at Lor talking fucking nonsense again."

I can hear you saying it as I write this. I know your voice so well, the way you'd intone rituals in your flat, soft, Mancunian accent. "O tha' circle, be tha' a meetin' place between the worlds ..." Karnayna became kaa-ney-ner, which always sounded both ridiculous and endearing. That's why it is a shock to hear your familiar smoky tones coming through the words of the book that Jimahl has written. At times it's just echoes, at other times it sounds as if you're right in the room. I can understand why Maxine said Jimahl's book gave her goosebumps.

"I am caught between the worlds," you told Jimahl, who read it as the lament of an earth-bound spirit impatient for the realms of the blessed. In it I hear the loneliness and frustration of a man walking by the sea so many years ago. "The path of a witch is the path of loneliness," you told me the first day we met. When I think of you now it's always as you were on that last day, when you were being scoured out, like those pieces of driftwood we were picking up on the shore, or an empty shell that chuckles in the ear. Perhaps I am being fanciful. Perhaps it is just wishful thinking, because I wish you were still around. But now it seems that you might be. Which is why I ask you, Alex, wherever you are, to remember that your friend Loriel kept faith till the end. Do me a favour, old friend, if there's any magick left in you, speak to us again.

Your friend,
Loriel

October 25, 2003 Sussex, England

Jimahl DiFiosa

A Voice in the Forest

Jimahl DiFiosa

PREFACE

If I were you, I'd be doing the same thing you're doing: reading the preface to try to find out who this guy 'Jimahl' is and what makes him think he really contacted Alex Sanders. After all, who the heck is Jimahl anyway? You've never run into him at festivals, he doesn't post to alt.pagan, and he hasn't appeared on talk radio or given Halloween interviews.

Jimahl joined my coven as a new student, though one with an impressive grasp of the Craft and a little experience in ceremonial magick. It was April 1988 and, as it turned out, less than two weeks before Alex Sanders passed through the veil. Since then, Jimahl has completed his training and then trained his own students, all the while doing what I — and every teacher — both fears and desires: surpassing his teacher. His rituals are full of poetry, beauty, and power; his insight on dreams and magickal mysteries — priceless. And if that weren't enough, he is a warm and witty person and one of my most trusted and dearest friends in the Craft.

He is also something quite rare these days: a 'natural' psychic and seer. So, it was no surprise to me that he would 'get' someone when using the spirit board one summer night while camping. And, strangely, it was simultaneously not surprising and the most incredible thing on earth to realize he was 'getting' Alex.

Alex Sanders, a controversial figure whose exploits were often trumpeted in the English tabloids, was chronicled in 1969 in King of the Witches by June Johns and approximately two years later in What Witches Do by Stewart Farrar. A natural magician with a flair for publicity and the dramatic, Alex was both reviled and praised for bringing witchcraft to the general public. His goal was to make it more accessible, which he certainly did, but detractors were horrified by his pandering to the press and his giving away of the Craft secrets.

A Voice in the Forest

When I met Alex in March of 1987, he was an older, calmer man, even frail. Gone was the arrogant showman of the late 60s and early 70s. He was pleasant, good-natured, and most sincere in his love of the goddess and his hopes for the future of the Craft. It was that
aspect of his personality that came through during the sessions described in this book. I am not sure how much of the Alex Sanders legend is true, and how much might be attributed to Alex's own exaggerations — Johns' book has some rather wild tales in it, as does Farrar's. But this I know: the communications Jimahl describes here happened. He has changed some of the names and physical descriptions of people and places to protect privacy, but these sessions did occur. And it is my strong belief that he contacted Alex, or at least some astounding entity capable of reading all our minds to find out not only what we were thinking of — and a few things we never even thought of — but all we knew of Alex. Then this incredible entity consistently imitated him, at our whim. Pretty hard work when the entity could have easily just told us it was a Being of Light from Mars.

If you're not an Alexandrian (that is, a follower of the particular tradition of witchcraft that Alex Sanders founded), you may wonder why these sessions are so important. The obvious answer would be that Alex has an important message about the goddess. Beyond that, there is something equally important. In this day of sheer materialism, these sessions
are profound because they are direct contact with the unknown, with that which has gone before, with the world beyond MTV, email, mass consumerism, and the evening news. This chronicle is something you can read, the whole while repeating to yourself: It's NOT a movie...

Because this is not just special effects. Because this is real.

Blessed Be.
Morven
August 29, 1999

Jimahl DiFiosa

A Voice in the Forest

Jimahl DiFiosa

INTRODUCTION

Alex Sanders, known in his lifetime as 'King of the Witches' and the founder of the Alexandrian tradition of Wicca, died in 1988. Alex, along with Gerald Gardner, remains one of the most imposing influences responsible for the resurgence of Wicca, or the Craft of the Wise, within the Twentieth Century.

He seemed determined from an early age to learn the Ancient Art of Witchcraft. His unique approach to Wicca, coupled with his tireless devotion to the Old Gods, created a new wave of interest in the Craft. It is a wave still cresting today as generations of new students step foot into a magick circle for the first time.

There were undoubtedly many covens operating at the time of his death that traced their lineage directly back to Alex. I was a member of one of these covens, Na Fineachan Glice located in eastern Massachusetts. When Alex first passed away in 1988, his spirit seemed extremely accessible during ritual. Many Alexandrians described a sense of his presence in their celebrations. This sensation seemed especially acute during initiation rituals when often the blindfolded postulate, poised on the brink of the ritual circle for the first time, would describe being embraced or kissed by 'someone' just before entering the consecrated space.

For a long while after his death, this acute awareness of Alex persisted, perhaps associated directly with our sense of loss. The wounds of his passing eventually healed. Time pressed on, each new season bringing another. Years went by. The family of NFG continued to grow and expand. To date, five new covens have been born of NFG and continue to thrive in the New England area.

A Voice in the Forest

Then, in one strange night, everything changed.

At Lammas in 1998, while camping in the forest of New Hampshire, a handful of NFG elders made a startling discovery. We were attempting to use a spirit board around the campfire one evening. In the illumination of the leaping fire, we decided to try to contact the spirit of Alex Sanders. To our surprise, a spirit readily established a strong connection with us and convincingly identified himself as Alex.

Over a period of many months, the communication with Alex continued. The documentation of our many sessions with the spirit board is adapted largely from Morven's meticulous notes. I have edited out the inevitable nonsense as the planchette began to move.

I have also eliminated information which was intended for specific individuals, and considered too personal to share publicly. The book you now hold in your hands is the result of our mutual efforts to document this remarkable story and to preserve Alex's messages. It is my hope that the spirit of Alex Sanders will touch your life as deeply as it has ours.

May the gods preserve the Craft.

Jimahl
Lammas 1999

Jimahl DiFiosa

Jimahl DiFiosa

Chapter One

A VOICE IN THE FOREST

A Voice in the Forest

Jimahl DiFiosa

Night is dark in the woods of New Hampshire, especially when the moon is barely past new. It is late July 1998. here are six of us camping together. Our tent sites, sheltered by evergreen and hardwood, are spaced randomly around the edges of a large field. In the daylight the spaces we inhabit are clearly visible from the field, but in the shadows it becomes difficult to find my way among the trees. I fumble with the branches at the edge of the woods, where I imagine I see a path. He sound of laughter drifts through the mass of shrubbery. It is enough of a lead for me to follow and a few moments later I make my way into the campsite carrying an arm load of firewood. Phoenix is kneeling on the stone ire ring, arranging a sizable stack of twigs into a pyramid.

"I'm going to build a ire," he declares with a smile.
I understand his excitement. We are from the city and this is an adventure for us. He accepts my humble offering of combustibles and goes back to his project. "It'll be my first ire," he says confidently.
"Well, make it a good one," I respond. "It's getting pretty damned cold out here tonight."
There is a picnic table near the ire pit and Morven is seated there. She is lighting candles from a box of candle stubs, one by
one, and placing them in the necks of empty bottles. hey illuminate the table erratically and the effect of the shifting light in the branches above us is eerie.

Morven is my teacher. I have studied the Craft with her for over a decade. Even now, although I am responsible for a coven of my own, she remains my closest friend in matters of the occult. I sit across from her and assist with the candles.
"Very elegant," I joke. She smiles.

There is a sense of timelessness to Morven. I remember the way she looked earlier in the day. I had found her walking in the woods wearing a

ritual robe and shawl. Except for her conventional eyeglasses, she looked as if she had stepped out of a fairy tale.
"Have you seen Raven and Jack?" she asks quietly. Before I can answer, there is the familiar sound of others making yet another path through the dark undergrowth. A couple emerges from the shadows, entering the campsite. Jack carries more wood and Phoenix accepts it gratefully.

"Make sure you get a lot of twigs and small stuff going first," Jack advises. I know he is familiar with building a ire, as I have spent many an evening lounging in front of the fireplace of the old farmhouse he shares with Raven.

"The lake is beautiful tonight," Raven says, taking a seat next to Morven at the picnic table. "And the stars…" She sighs and pulls her woolen cloak close around her. Of all of us, she is the only one who brought something warm to wear. It's obvious she's a pro at camping. She thinks of everything. "It's July — almost August, for that matter. Why is it so cold?" I'm not really complaining, just saying out loud what everyone else is thinking.

"The cold keeps the mosquitoes away," Jack says, matter of factly. He comes over to the table and sits down next to his wife. Jack seems as tall and slender as a sapling. Raven leans into his embrace. "It'll be better when Phoenix gets the ire going," Morven says loudly enough for Phoenix to hear. And true to his pronouncement, the first sputter of ire is heard behind us. He smell of the smoke drifts to us like incense — and mixes in our senses with the sounds of the forest around us.

"Now wait until the ire catches hold," Jack coaches, "then add some of the smaller logs." Phoenix is dancing around the ire pit like a conjurer — the glow of the ire illuminates his muscular body. He begins to recite aloud a centuries-old invocation to the elemental spirits. I watch him happily. He is my student, and it is exciting to see him revel in such a primitive setting. "He's done it," I call out, and Phoenix beams back at me from beyond the brand new tower of lame. "Congratulations!"

The trail of ire twists and turns upward, in a few magick moments transforming the campsite into a ring of golden light.
Paul emerges sleepily from the tent where he has been resting. He rubs his eyes, as if the campfire was the first light of morning.

"What's all the shouting about?" he asks and, before an answer can be offered, adds, "Anything let to eat? I'm hungry."
Paul joins Phoenix for a moment at the fireside. I watch the two of them laughing at the roar of the ire.

Morven takes her cue from Paul and slips into the extra tent where our communal food is stored. She returns with two paper shopping bags overflowing with junk food. Cookies, potato chips, pretzels, cheese, and crackers all spill out onto the picnic table.
As if by magick, Jack produces a bottle of wine from the shadows. he cork is dislodged easily and the wine is poured into paper cups. I sit at the table and watch my friends by candlelight. I think of how complete my life seems at this moment. The sound of their laughter, the fireruddied complexion of their faces, and the fine crackling of the campfire become images that I consciously try to burn into my memory.

Remember this when you're back at the office. Remember the earth beneath your bare feet and the smell of the burning wood.

I don't remember who mentioned it first, but at this point it was suggested that we play with the spirit board that Paul had packed. I had joked with him as we struggled to sort all of our gear into manageable portions. Paul was known for over-packing. "What self-respecting witch is going camping without their spirit board?" he argued. He won.

The familiar box is retrieved from his tent and set up on the picnic table. We have to move the junk food to the side to make room for the board. "Who's up first?" I ask, meaning, of course, who would work the planchette. I guess I am misunderstood to be volunteering. Paul sits down opposite me and says something like "I'll give it a try with you."

Morven picks up a damp notebook and a pen that had been used earlier in the day to drat a grocery list. This proves to be a good idea, as Morven is able to take fast and accurate notes. She sits down closest to the campfire for better visibility, and just happens to be the farthest away from the spirit board. he others place themselves between Morven and the board and we wait patiently for something to happen. We don't have a long wait, as a response to our question comes rapidly.

"Is anybody there?" I ask.
The planchette stirs with an audible groan and moves across the board. It is actually creaking like a rusty hinge as it moves.

"Is anybody there?" Again, cautiously, the planchette races to a word printed in the corner of the board.

YES

"Who is this?" I continue. Paul is looking at me as if to say "I'm not moving it, are you?" I return an equally puzzled expression and watch the planchette spell out:

Q U E S T I O N M E

"Are you telling us to ask a question?"

YES

"Tell us who you are."
The planchette continues to move in an awkward creaking way — it seems as if we are communicating with a very old spirit. here is a series of nonsensical responses. I get impatient and threaten to

dismiss the spirit.

"We're going to let you go if you don't start making sense," I warn.

NO

"Are you a spirit?" someone asks.

J IN

"Are you telling us you're a djinn?" Morven asks.

YES

"You're a ire elemental king?" I pose a clumsy question as I try to remember what I had read about the structure of the Elemental Kingdoms.

NO

"You're a ire elemental, though?"

YES

"Have you come because of the ire that Phoenix built?"

YES

"Tell us about ire elementals."

YO U S E E M E

"Where — in the ire?"

YES

A Voice in the Forest

"Are you a genii?"

YES

"What other elementals are here?"

E A R TH

"Is there anything you can share with us as witches?"

W E C O M E W H E N W E R C A L L D

"We have the ability to summon?"

YES

"hat's because we are witches?"

BE L I E V E

"Because we believe?"

YES

We speak for a few more minutes with the djinn and then Phoenix and Raven are anxious to try the planchette. Paul and I relinquish our positions gladly.

Unfortunately, the planchette doesn't move at all for the two of them, and after a few frustrated attempts, Raven asks if Jack will give it a try with her. It seems logical that the two of them would have good results. Raven asks most of the questions this time around.

"Is someone here?"

                    YES

"Were you there just a minute ago and not answering?"

                    NO

"What is your name?"

                    AT I C

"Do you mean an attic like in a house?"

                    AT I C YES

"Are you from our attic?"

                    YES

"What are you?"

                    D ED

"Are you a spirit of a dead person?"

                    YES

"Did you come camping with us?"

                    YES

"Did you see me take the camping stuff out of the attic?"

A Voice in the Forest

YES

"When you were alive, did you live in our house?"

"Tell us who you are."

YES

To the mutual surprise of Raven and Jack, the entity proceeds to spell out the name of a former resident of their old house — a ghost that has been seen in their home several times. They laugh nervously and the session ends abruptly.
The idea that their household ghost decided to go camping with Raven and Jack seems funny and we all have a good laugh about it.

We continue our entertainment for a while longer with minimal results, trying many variations on the partnering. Then someone suggests that Paul and I take a turn again. Morven would later write: "Paul and Jimahl were on the planchette again. I was transcribing. Paul and Jimahl decided they wanted to try to contact Alex Sanders. We all agreed that they give it a try since they seem to make a good team. Where I could remember who said what, I've noted it; however, the planchette moved so fast that evening that I barely had time to transcribe, so I couldn't always note who said what. I could, however, remember what I said, so you'll see my name a lot. I think that Jimahl was asking most of the questions in this session. An interesting note: In the irst group of sessions, the planchette creaked. During this session, the planchette did not creak. his was unusual."

"We would like to contact Alex and only Alex. Is Alex Sanders available to communicate with us?"
"Alex, is this you?"

YES
5 KI S

Morven recognizes the abbreviation for the ive-fold kiss — a traditional Wiccan greeting. "Alex, you give us the ivefold kiss?"

YES

"Alex, is this really you?"

YES

"You haven't reincarnated yet?"

NO

"Why are you staying on the astral?"

2000

"You're staying until the year 2000?"

YES

"Is that okay with you?"

YES

"Alex, do you remember Morven?"

YES

"Any special message for her?"

TEACH THEM TO LOVE GODESS

At this point, we are all staring at each other like deer caught in the headlights. My fingertips are trembling slightly on the planchette next to Paul's. There is a tremendous amount of excitement in the air and it is difficult to concentrate on keeping the connection. I seem to remember a pause here where everyone takes a deep breath. I then decide to present the entity with a qualifying test to make sure this is indeed Alex.

"Alex, do you mind being tested?"

NO

Since Morven is the only one present who had actually met Alex, I ask her to devise a test for him.

Morven later wrote: "I was thinking about the last time I saw Alex. He was sitting in a large stuffed chair, facing me, smiling, with a glass of white wine in his right hand. I thought to myself: Alex, all you have to do is say 'white' or 'wine' — either one — it's not hard. I write the words 'white wine' on the top right corner of the paper on which I am taking notes. I remember that I tap Jack, who is on my right, on the arm and point to the words. He nods. No one to my let — Jimahl or Paul — can see this because it's extremely dark (new moon) and there are boxes of crackers and snacks between the notebook and them. No one notices that Jack looks at the notebook and nods."

I am very anxious at this point to ind out if this is really Alex. My head is filled with images of him. I have a very strange feeling that we are really onto something that would reshape all of our lives in ways we could not possibly comprehend.

Come on, Alex, say something.... I have no idea of what sort of test Morven has devised. No one is saying anything. he moment seems to hang there forever and then the planchette starts to move again...

WI N E

"Wine!" Paul calls out. He spells out the word, "w-i-n-e."

Morven shows us the words on her notebook and speaks them aloud, as it is so dark that we have trouble reading her notes, even when they are right in front of our eyes. The campfire has died down into embers and there is only the candlelight from two tapers and a couple of citronella buckets.

There is a short pause in the process while people gasp in awe.

Morven would later note: "Jimahl and Paul admirably keep their hands on the planchette and maintain their composure. I am concurrently in complete shock that this happened and yet at the same time feel that this is absolutely normal and why should I be surprised... I mutter a silent thank you to Alex and suggest we continue."

"Alex, is this really you?" I am remembering Alex's death in 1988. I was a new student of the Craft at the time. I calculate quickly. *He's been dead for ten years. Ten years!*

YES

"You've been there all along?"

YES

I ask if anyone has any questions. Morven suggests one. "Who is Azarak?"

H O RN E D 1

Morven suggests another question. "Who is Zomelak?" (Note: Azarak and Zomelak are two archaic names used in the traditional 'Witches Rune.' here seems to be an ongoing academic debate as to their origin.)

S U N G OD

A Voice in the Forest

"Azarak and Zomelak are god names?"

YES

"Alex, are you happy with us?"

YES

"What can you tell us about our coven family?"

G RO W

"Are you with us when we cast a circle?"

M OS T

"You're with us most of the time?"

YES

"Who initiated you?" his question comes from Morven.

R A I S E D 1F R E D

"Is 'Fred' someone's mundane name?"

YES

"Can you tell us about magick?"

W O RS H I P

"Magick is worship?"

Jimahl DiFiosa

GODS

"Worship the gods and goddesses?"

YES

The questions were coming from the group as quickly as Alex's responses now. Someone asks. "What is it like later you die?"

DREAM

"You mean it's surreal?" Raven asks.

YES

"Was your work finished when you passed?"

READY

"Did you leave anything unfinished?"

YES

"What?"

GIFT

"A gift you meant to give?"

YES

"Who was the gift for?"

STUDENTS

A Voice in the Forest

"Which students?"

ALL

"What was the gift?"

BOOKS

"You mean you had other books?"

YES

"Were they already written when you died?"

U KNOW

"You're saying we know about these books?"

YES

"Is there anything else you want to share?"

HI L U V

"Are you talking to Morven?"

YES

Morven later remarked that Alex used to say "Hi, luv" to people when he met them — including her.

"Do you have a message for each of us?"

YES

Jimahl DiFiosa

For the next quarter hour or so, Alex proceeds to deliver a series of personal messages to each of us who are present, and many people not present who are part of our extended Wiccan family. Each of the messages is concise, almost cryptic.

Some consist of a mantra-like sentence of one or two words, but when delivered to those for whom they were intended, many of the messages will have a profound effect. In many cases, Alex will seem to have addressed a particular need of that individual, but which they have never articulated to anyone else.

For example, to someone who had stopped formally practicing the Craft over a decade ago, Alex says simply:

C O M E B A CK

What surprises Morven is not only the appropriateness of each message, but in many cases, the typical witty Alex sense of humor. To one of our group who is an eternal optimist, Alex says:

M A G I C I S G R E A T

We laugh because we could actually hear the person saying that. Alex has picked up on this person's personality. And, finally, to someone who has been very outwardly anxious recently, Alex says:

C A L M D O WN

In the months to come, many of the messages that were received from Alex would begin to unfold in a prophetic way within the context of our individual lives. We would ind ourselves reflecting again and again on his words — finding new meaning in them each time — like a complex and rare lower with petals removed only to reveal another layer of petals.

When Alex has nearly exhausted us all, we ask if he has a message for our entire Wiccan family. There are a few dozen of us now, all proudly tracing our lineage to Alex through Morven. He answers:

TO GET HERNES S

Morven puzzles over the response for a few seconds — spelling it out phonetically. It doesn't make sense.

"To get Herne's S?" Morven questions, perhaps visualizing the horned god of the forest.

NO (his was a most emphatic "No!")

"Alex, we don't understand, can you spell that again?" I ask. And the planchette moves patiently to the center of the board and begins to spell very slowly.

Morven copies every letter again, this time not trying to guess the spacing.

TOGETHERNESS

"Togetherness!" we call out simultaneously, laughing at how we could miss something so obvious.

And then he is gone.

... I don't remember what happened next. We all seemed to shuffle off to our tents mumbling to ourselves. What began as a game of amusement had ended with the opening of a door onto the astral which provided a substantial glimpse of a man who had previously existed to me only in books and other people's anecdotes. Now Alex seemed very real to me. He knew me, he spoke directly to me. And the words that had tumbled out through the planchette now rattled within my mind — What books is he talking about? What is it we are supposed to know? Who's Fred?

Jimahl DiFiosa

I climb into my sleeping bag and lay there for a long while before drifting of into a deep sleep.

"Togetherness," I whisper into the darkness.

And now the only response comes from the great pine tree that seems to sigh above my tent.

Jimahl DiFiosa

o—o

Chapter Two

NECROMANCY

A Voice in the Forest

Jimahl DiFiosa

It had been three months since the camping trip. The time went by quickly and there was little contact with any of the others. I thought of that night often, remembering (as I had promised myself) the smell of the fire, the wavering light of the candles, and the cold earth beneath my feet. But mostly my thoughts were of Alex. His 'voice' haunted me, waking and sleeping, and I felt very strongly that if we tried again, he would return to us and continue his communication.

Raven and Jack had invited me, along with Paul and Phoenix, to a Fall Equinox ritual and we had all accepted enthusiastically. It was an unbearably hot day for September and I found myself wandering through Raven's herb garden looking for a sheltered place to rest. I settled down on an old stone wall beneath an apple tree and closed my eyes. The last July days of summer swam back into my consciousness. I re-membered that before returning from the camping trip, we had gone to a secluded field and built an altar to Lugh, the dying sun god, and invoked him in the final glorious days of the season of light.

"The sacrificial king," I sighed, and the face of Alex Sanders came into my mind so vividly that I nearly fell from the wall.
The ritual was seasonably appropriate but strangely unsettling to me. I was admittedly preoccupied, worrying about my beloved familiar, for the beautiful black cat's health had been failing in the previous weeks. Feeling edgy during the feast, I was pulled aside by Raven, who asked me what was wrong.

"No one has mentioned Alex," I said.

"Bring the spirit board to Samhain." She laughed. "We'll have a chat with him then."
I puzzled over this for a moment. As a witch, it seemed odd to relegate matters of spirit communication only to Halloween. But I let it

drop.

I went home in a sullen mood to care for my dying cat. In fulfillment of my worst fears, his life slipped away and he was gone. I was devastated. We had spent twelve years together. It is part of the season. Let it go. But it left me with an emptiness that I found hard to shake.

Autumn came down rapidly and then lingered. The leaves on the trees in the Boston Common changed color quickly and then hung for days on the wet branches, as they twisted in the slightest breeze but would not fall. I watched them from the window of my office, trying to concentrate on business. It was nearly impossible, for the tide of All-Hallows was rising from the earth like a flood, and it threatened to pull me in head first. The messages from Alex had been delivered safely to those he had chosen. They elicited mixed emotions — from stunned silence; to tears; to denial, perhaps; to the most delirious joy. Even today, as I try to concentrate on other people's business, I am pondering my own message. Alex had told me to study. Or so I thought, for in the darkness he had spelled out 's-t-ud' and the planchette had faltered. Someone had called out "study" and the planchette moved to 'yes.' My message was certainly less spiritual than many of the others that I had been asked to deliver, but I took it to a humble heart and resolved to study more than ever the ways of the Craft. I loved books and collected them relentlessly. They were stacked everywhere in my small apartment. But I bought them faster than I could read them. Perhaps Alex, the perpetual scholar, was prompting me to become more diligent in my approach to learning.

The phone on my desk rings loudly, pulling me out of my own private thoughts. It is Paul.
"Two days," he says flatly. I look at my desk calendar. It is October 29. "Are we still on for that dinner party?" We have devised a language of codes that is appropriate for business environments.
"Wouldn't miss it." I laugh. "Did you remember to invite Alex?"

"Oh, yes. I hope he can make it. It's been a while since we've spoken with him."

We speak for a few moments more and then say good-bye.

Food for the dead, I scribble on a slip of paper and then, as an afterthought, I write beneath it coffee and eggs. I tuck it into my shirt pocket. "One- stop grocery shopping," I say aloud and make a mental note to stop at the market on the way home.
Paul, Phoenix, and I have decided to attempt to contact Alex again through the ancient rite of necromancy. We are a confident coven and our group soul is strong. We anticipate that we will be successful. We can sense Alex nearby, waiting patiently for an opportunity to finish that Lammas conversation. I make a silent promise to him that he will always be welcome in our circles. And as sure as a phoenix, in these last days of October, the power of the Craft rises again in my heart like a dark flame.
It is an hour or so before midnight on October 31, 1998. I gather my ritual tools into a worn backpack and walk the few blocks to Phoenix and Paul's apartment. The urban landscape is noisy with revelers. They brush past me in twos and threes, gather in the brightly lit doorways of buildings, and wait in line in costume to enter the neighborhood bar. We each keep the season in our own way. I ring the doorbell.

Paul greets me at the door and I enter the darkened apartment. Phoenix is lighting the last of the quarter candles. The smell of incense hangs heavily in the air. They are already robed and I quickly shed my own mundane clothing and pull on my ritual robe. I meet them in the kitchen where Paul is putting the finishing touches on the Dumb Supper, a traditional feast which is offered to the dead. I have baked some bread and I add it to the platter of food on the table.

We do not speak. Our mutual sense of purpose is obvious. I glance at the clock on the kitchen wall — it presses on toward the witching hour and we silently resolve to begin. A ceremonial circle has been marked out on the living room floor. An altar is ready on its western edge. It contains four plates, four chalices, a vase of red roses, and a photograph of Alex. We have surrounded it with our Books of Shadows, copied by hand from our initiators, as is the Alexandrian tradition. A censer of necromantic incense burns steadily. We made the incense together at the last Full Moon — the complex ingredients included three drops of blood, one from each of us. With one heart, we begin to prepare the temple.

"Before us, Raphael," Paul intones.

"Behind us, Gabriel," I add solemnly. I am facing the altar that we have built for Alex and above it hangs a large black mirror. Oddly, it does not reflect any of us and I make a mental note to share this observation with the others afterward.

"On our right hand, Michael," Phoenix says strongly. "On our left hand, Uriel."

The ritual continues as planned. Each word, each gesture, is loaded with our intent.

"I invoke ye angels of the celestial spheres," Phoenix is saying, "whose dwelling is in the invisible. Ye are the guardians of the gates of the universe. Be ye also the guardians of the gates of this mystic sphere." As we begin to raise the ancient tide of power, it seems as if we transcend the confines of a Boston apartment and are standing within a temple so vast that the parameters of it blur into imagination. Our candles flame brightly against the dark and our voices resonate confidently in the still hour of mid-night.
Paul is walking backward, in the way of the dead, carrying our incense and two white candles to the west of our circle. He kneels before the photo of Alex and lights the tapers from the western candle. Alex's face seems to leap into animation from within the glass frame. Phoenix follows in the same manner. He carries red wine. Finally, I follow, moving slowly in the same backward manner bearing our solemn supper of pale cheese, freshly baked bread, apples, and clusters of purple grapes.

We wait for a few moments before continuing. My heart seems ready to jump out of my chest. I am anxious. I sense that the others are, too. Finally, Paul breaks the tension and takes a single rose from the vase.

He lays it across Alex's plate and says quietly:

"I welcome you, Alex Sanders, King of the Witches. Be with us now." Phoenix fills Alex's chalice to overflowing with the wine. It sparkles in the candlelight and stains the white tablecloth.

"I welcome you, Alex Sanders, our spiritual father. Be with us now."

I take small amounts of food and arrange them next to the rose. "Spirit of Alex Sanders," I continue, my voice wavering, "you may now approach the gates of the West. Arise, arise, I charge you. Be with us now."

I look into the mirror which hangs directly above our heads, over Alex's plate. It is foggy and a mist swirls across its surface.

"Spirit of Alex Sanders deceased, you may now pass beyond the gates of the West and enter our circle. Arise, arise, I charge you. Be with us now. We welcome you, Alex Sanders, by the ties of love that bind us, to break your eternal fast and sup with us. So mote it be!"
In the months that follow this evening, we will all have different memories of what happened next. Paul describes looking down and seeing Alex physically standing before him. "I saw his bare feet and the hem of a white robe, trimmed with gold. He was as solid as we were. I did not feel as if I should look up into his face so I just stared at his feet. He stood just inside of the circle."

Phoenix saw him in the black mirror — he stood in the forefront of a crowd of other departed souls. "The ritual attracted many other spirits," he would tell me afterward. "They all wanted to come inside. Alex stood in the front of the crowd — he looked right at me."

A Voice in the Forest

I was glad that I had followed my instincts and decided to take an added precaution at the last minute. We had agreed that we would not breach the circle in any way. Although it seemed inappropriate to command Alex's spirit into the traditional 'triangle of manifestation' used in necromancy, it seemed equally unwise to cut the circle to allow Alex to enter. Because of the other spirits attending, this proved to be a good decision. We believed strongly that Alex would be capable of transcending our magickal boundary.

I sensed Alex come into the circle and take his seat at the feast. I do remember that Paul was acting strangely. He kept staring at the floor and would not look up. Phoenix noticed this also and looked at me inquisitively. "He shuddered," I would later comment. "His whole body convulsed for a second. It was as if Alex passed through him when he entered the circle." We sit in silence for a while, each communing with Alex in our own quiet way and then Phoenix suggests we try the spirit board again. Paul and I take the planchette. Phoenix acts as scribe. Although no questions have been asked yet, the planchette moves quickly to:

YES

"Do you have a message for us? A spell to teach us?" Phoenix asks. He would later remark that he sensed that Alex wanted to instruct us in some manner of the occult.

F L Y YES

"A flying spell?" I ask nervously "How? We are earthbound. How can we learn to fly?"

D YE

The attempt to spell 'die' leaves us all feeling a little weird. Of course we had just walked in the path of the dead and were clearly out of our usual

element. Then I ask something like:
"Alex, are you making a joke? Are you saying that to learn a flying spell you must die?" The planchette moves weakly and spells:

S E E R S YES

"Do you want to teach us to be seers?"

NO D J I N

Phoenix, remembering the camping retreat, asks if Alex is referring to scrying by fire.

YES C A U L D R O N

"Alex, are you saying this is a good time to invoke the element of fire for scrying?"

YES

Paul and I stare at each other across the board. He seems distant and I start to worry that we are all too tired to be doing this type of thing. The connection to Alex feels different this time, very strained. There is a heavy feeling in the air — like we are wrapped in wet fabric.

"Alex," I press on, "can you tell us more about the messages you gave us at Lammas?"

H E E D T H E M W E L L YES

"Alex, I need some clarification on my message. You started to spell a word but did not finish."

YES

A Voice in the Forest

"Was the word study?"

The planchette moves painfully slowly now and Alex be-gins to spell:

S T U D ...

Then, to my surprise, the completed word expands to:

S T UDEN T S

"Students!" I laugh out loud, realizing how I had spent three months contemplating my erroneous interpretation of his message. "My current students?" I ask, meaning Paul and Phoenix.

N O MO RE

"Alex, I am finished teaching for now. My students now have students. I need a break."

NOT A K E M O R E I H A D H U N D R E D S YES

This is a humbling response. I am speechless.
"Alex?" Paul asks, "Your message to me was to heal others. How can I do this?"

HA N DS

"Alex, I have had no experience with healing. How can I heal with my hands?"

T O UC H

"You're saying this is my spiritual talent?"

YES

"Is there anything else, Alex?" Paul asks.

NO

"Did you enjoy the supper?" I ask.

YES A B S O R B

And then without warning the planchette moves to:

GOODBYE

At this point we all feel him leave and the circle seems to immediately grow colder. I sense a familiar draft about my ankles that always comes as the power wanes.

We each retrace the path of the dead, this time moving out of the realm of the departed into the world of the living.

As we inhabit the last vestiges of our Samhain circle, I thank Alex for hearing our call and invoke the Most Ancient Goddess into our temple. "O Mighty Mother," I pray, "wake the witch in us. Set a fire ablaze in our hearts for the love of the Craft. Empower us with your dark magick!"

Paul is standing next to me. He smiles and nods. Phoenix embraces me and says, "Now that was a ritual to remember! I think we've all earned a beer!"

The next morning I awake to the sound of the telephone. It is Phoenix.

"Paul is very sick," he says urgently. "Can you come over here now? I don't know what to do."

Because Phoenix is not the type of individual who easily gets excited, and for intuitive reasons of my own, I believe that Paul's situation must be extremely grave. I dress rapidly and run the few blocks to their apartment.

"Thanks for coming," Phoenix says as he opens the door. "I didn't know who else to call!"

I enter the dark apartment. Although it is a bright morning, the shades are all drawn. It takes a moment for my eyes to adjust.
"Where is he?" I ask. Phoenix points to Paul's bedroom door, which is closed. "What's wrong with him?"

"I don't know. We stayed up a while last night after you left. He seemed to be fine. But this morning he won't get out of bed."

I walk to the bedroom door and knock once. There is no answer. I push the door open and walk into the room. Many years previously I had worked as a security guard in a hospital. I remember clearly now the curious smell that pervaded the rooms of terminally ill patients. It was a sweet, dark smell — like flowers on the ebb. I am startled to smell it now, filling Paul's bedroom. He lies under a thin bedsheet, which is pulled up to just below his chest. The first thing I notice is that he is so pale — his flesh is the color of day-old snow. He has a cloth over his eyes and if he noticed me enter the room, he does not acknowledge my presence. Phoenix comes in behind me and looks at me expectantly. It is at times like this that I wish desperately for an Official High Priest Manual to consult. So much of the occult has to be learned the hard way.

"Paul," I whisper, "can you hear me?" "I hurt," he says faintly. His voice raises the hair on the back of my neck. It is not his voice.
"Every part of me hurts. I feel like I'm dying."
"You're not dying. What's wrong?"
"I don't understand," he says in a raspy voice. "I have never felt this sick in my life."

I look at Phoenix, who stares back at me. My mind quickly flashes back to the previous evening.

"We did everything right," I murmur. "By the book. What could have gone wrong?" I then instinctively know what is wrong, but denial feels pretty good at this particular moment.
"Let's get him into the living room," I say to Phoenix.

We move to either side of Paul and try to get him out of the bed. He stands up weakly, wavering on his feet as if he's about to break into pieces. We half-walk, half-drag him into the living room and lay him down in the center of the floor.

"Get some pillows for his head," I instruct Phoenix.
I wrestle with the shades on the windows and an unapoloetic light floods the room. Paul moans and covers his eyes with his hands.

Paul, usually as solid and fit as a young Viking, lies on the bare floor clad only in a pair of gray shorts. His blond hair is streaked with sweat, his blue eyes clouded. I am having an adrenaline rush. I have no idea what is physically wrong with my friend, but my hunch is that it has something to do with Alex. I glance at my watch and figure that I have a ten-minute window to try to make things right — before I suggest to Phoenix that we call an ambulance.

"Bring the salt and water from the altar," I say to Phoenix. Then I begin to bathe Paul's feet with the consecrated water from our ritual. His body seems to wither as each painful moment slips by.
"This is an illusion," I tell Phoenix. "This isn't really happening. Bathe his forehead with the consecrated water." Phoenix does so, but still I watch the flesh on Paul's body pull taut. I can see every rib now! I am on the verge of panic. I try to remember every detail of the ritual. Something went wrong. Then I recall what happened at the moment Alex came into the circle. Paul had shuddered involuntarily — his whole body shook. Instinctively, I realize that Paul had not only been the watcher of the western gate — he had inadvertently become the gate. Alex had passed through him into the circle.

"Think!" I say to Phoenix. "What do we know about necromancy?"
"Historically it was used to reanimate the corpse," Phoenix says. I can see that his concern for Paul's health is magnifying.
"Right, but we knew that wasn't going to be the case with Alex. So we raised his spirit — not in hypothetical form — but his actual ghost — for lack of a better word."

"Get to the point," Phoenix says urgently. "What do we do now?"
"I think Alex literally passed into Paul and then through him into the circle. But some aspect of Alex remains."

"Remains where?" Phoenix asks impatiently.
I nod in Paul's direction. "In there — inside Paul." "So what do we do?"

"Alex, we love you and honor you," I say, "but we realize that somehow a part of your spirit became lodged in Paul. This is causing Paul's body to take on the physical form you knew in the last hours of your life. He is reliving your illness, Alex. He is feeling your pain. You have to help us, Alex."

Paul begins to cry — great heaving sobs that shake his whole body. Suddenly his torso, from chest to toe, is raised from the floor and bent backward like a bow.
"Alex, for the love of the goddess, let go of Paul. Now!"
Paul's body slams back to the floor.

He lies still for more than a few minutes and then opens his eyes and looks directly at me. I recognize the familiar light there.
"Let's just stick with the spirit board," he says, and we all laugh.

Jimahl DiFiosa

Jimahl DiFiosa

Chapter Three

THE SECOND GROUP SESSION

A Voice in the Forest

Jimahl DiFiosa

It is a week later and the three of us are together again — this time in Paul's car heading out of Boston toward Raven and Jack's covenstead. If the leaves on the trees in the city were reluctant to fall, just the opposite is true in the suburbs north of town. The wet branches show little signs of life and the landscape is uninviting. A low ground-fog rises up on either side of the two-lane blacktop and adds to the dreary atmosphere. Paul inches up the steep hill that leads to the covenstead, his high-beams barely illuminating the pavement ahead of us.

"A great night for a ghost hunt," Phoenix jokes.
The evening promises to be entertaining. Raven and Jack own one of the most haunted houses in New England. Four ghosts had been documented there to date — one of whom we had encountered at Lammas. The other resident spirits include a mysterious gardener (never seen inside the house, but always anxious to dispense gardening advice to unsuspecting guests on the patio), an energetic two-year-old named Edward, and the spirit of a woman who frequently awakened house guests in the morning by calling out their names.

Because so many members of our Wiccan family have young children who enjoy trick or treating, this annual ritual has been deliberately scheduled a week past actual Halloween to facilitate attendance.
"Is everyone going to be there?" I ask from the back seat, where I am surrounded by pillows and sleeping bags. Since the ritual was scheduled to begin at midnight, Raven had suggested we sleep over afterward.
"I think we'll have a full house," Paul responds, still focusing intently on the foggy highway. "I got last-minute emails from five of them reminding me to bring the spirit board."

"I hope Alex will join us," I respond. There is a moment of silence and I realize we are all thinking of the necromancy experiment.
"So what the hell happened last weekend?" Phoenix finally asks. "I think

it should have been an expected side effect. I suppose there is an inherent danger of possession in any spirit work." I had given the situation some thought in the last few days.

Paul laughs nervously. "Possession?"

"I don't mean possession in a head-spinning way," I explain, "but I think it's somewhat natural for disembodied spirits to gravitate toward a warm body."

"Like the impulse to get in out of the cold," Phoenix says. "Exactly," I continue, "but the fact that Alex sort of hung around with Paul for a while could be symptomatic of something else."

The farmhouse suddenly seems to float into view as Paul's vehicle rounds the top of the steep hill. Set against a field of night, the lights of the many windows glow like the eyes of a huge jack-o-lantern. Paul parks the car at the edge of a crowded driveway and turns off the engine. We sit there for a moment in the dark.

"You were saying?" Paul smiles.

"Just call it a hunch, but I don't think Alex has passed through the veil. I assumed he was speaking to us from the other side, but now I think his spirit may still be earthbound."

The front door of the house swings open and from across the yard a blade of yellow light illuminates a flagstone path. A cloaked figure moves toward us. We step out of the car into the cold November air. The sound of a distant violin, its music drifting upon the wind, surprises us.

Raven throws her arms up to greet us. "Welcome, welcome," she says. Her long black hair blows in the wind. Her cat circles her ankles. We make our way into the house quickly and shut the door against the damp chill.

The house takes the three of us in quickly, embracing us as only an old house can. Morven is there, looking radiant in the firelight, curled up elegantly on the sofa. A vigorous fire is blazing in the massive stone hearth and the music of the violin fills the room completely.

Sulis is standing in front of the fire, her back as straight as a door, the instrument cradled against her chin, her head thrown back in the rapture of the music. Her long red hair falls over her shoulders and dances like the flames on the hearth. The music is passionate, sad in a way, but only in that enigmatic way that makes one happy to be sad. She sways from side to side as she plays, lost in the bittersweet notes that she is creating. When she finishes with a flourish, there is applause and warm words from the others.
"Jimahl," she calls out when she sees me, and we kiss.

Jack comes into the room from the kitchen carrying a large bowl of candy. "Leftovers from last weekend." He laughs.

I decline the offer and pass by him to enter the kitchen. The aromas that drift from the oven are intoxicating — sweet cinnamon, crisp apple, and the smell of baking bread. A pot of stew simmers on top of the cast-iron stove. Willow leans over it holding a wooden spoon.

"I could use some rosemary," she says as I enter. I take a few pinches of the herb from bunches of drying plants that hang in front of Raven's antique china cabinet. Willow accepts the requested ingredient from me and drops it into the mixture.

"Rosemary for remembrance." She smiles.

"I was hoping you'd be here," I say as I embrace her warmly. She leans into me, her body is as soft as a pillow.

I consider Willow to be my Wiccan sister. We became students to Morven at the same time and grew into the Craft together. Just as two trees, planted beside each other, may appear to be independent above the ground and yet share the same piece of earth, their roots intermingled, so was my relationship with Willow intertwined. After years spent walking the same path, life circumstances eventually separated us. It had been a year or more since we stood in the same room. Willow sighs loudly, speaking volumes in her sighs. She is the living embodiment of the axiom that still waters run deep.

Ruanna comes into the kitchen from the back yard. She is younger in the Craft than Willow and I, having come to Morven for instruction much later, but there is an aura of antiquity to Ruanna. Witchcraft seems to cover her like a mantle and she wears it well. A scarlet tattoo of a rising sun blazes beautifully over her heart.
"We're all set up in the carriage house," she announces. "We've just got to get a few more logs into the wood burning stove. It's cold out there." As if on cue, Morph comes in from the living room carrying an armload of firewood.

"Did someone mention wood?" He laughs. Perhaps it is the magician's robe, its hem dotted with stars and moons, but Morph seems to me like a young Merlin tonight. He is per-haps the most intellectual person that I know. He is to be found, more often than not, settled into a comfortable chair with a book in his lap and his eyeglasses balanced precariously at the end of his nose.

"Is everyone here?" Ruanna asks. "It's getting close to mid-night." There is the sound of footsteps again in the foyer and a fresh round of "hellos."

It is Tanith. She is the true elder among us, having been instrumental in the training of Morven. Tanith is ageless in the way that most Wiccan women become — with features as fine as porcelain and long, slender hands that seem to weave patterns in the air when they move.

"What a warm welcome," Tanith says, as she patiently hugs each one of us. "Oh dear, there are so many of you. How exciting! Happy Samhain. Blessed be!"

Jimahl DiFiosa

When all has settled again, Raven announces that it is time to begin the ritual. We drift off into adjoining rooms to complete our individual preparations. I robe quickly and draw a black cloak around my shoulders. The others have already started to form a procession. I join them and together we move silently from the warmth of the living room, through the bright kitchen, and open the heavy door that leads out from the rear of the house. We cross the broad expanse of wet grass in our bare feet. Our cloaks and robes billow in the wind.

The door of the carriage house is open and candlelight beckons invitingly from inside. We enter quickly and the door is shut behind us. It takes a moment for my eyes to adjust to the dim light. A large circle is drawn out on the plank floor. An altar, overflowing with produce from Raven's garden, is set up at the edge of this circle.
There are candles everywhere, set around the perimeter of the space — spilling lavishly across the altar, and flickering slyly from inside carved pumpkins, which ring the room like enchanted sentinels. An old potbellied stove dominates one corner of the renovated space. The heat from the stove fogs the windows and makes the rough wooden floor warm be-neath our feet. The smell of burning hardwood is a heady incense.

"As the wheel of the year slows, the cycle of change pulls us into dark, cool spaces," Jack proclaims as he walks slowly around the circle. "The leaves fall from the trees — orange and red — to the earth below where they become as we all must become — dust — a part of the dark, wet void from which surges the cosmic impulse of regeneration."

We join hands and begin to dance slowly— swaying from side to side as Morph keeps time on a hollow drum. Jack begins the invocation.

"Dark Lady, by want so keen, it cuts like knife. By heart of green as sharp as scythe.

I call thee forth, O Queen of Night.
By waning light of silver moon,

A Voice in the Forest

By breath of night I chant this rune. By darkness deep I know thee nigh;
By wind and rain and lowering sky. By circle round we weave your spell.
Shake and shudder, shriek and scream, Phantom Mother, Shadow Queen."

Raven appears suddenly in the shadows of the altar. She wears a dark red veil which hangs low across her face.
"This is the time for scrying," she says, "for looking into black mirrors and divining with the tarot. The veil between the living and the dead is lifted for a moment. Let us now commune with those who have gone before. Let us see our own future in the shadows between the worlds."

As we sprawl out in the center of the large circle, a shared excitement begins to build. Although there are plenty of runes, tarot cards, and dark crystal spheres to utilize, Raven suggests that Paul and I try to contact Alex on the spirit board. The board is brought out and we all sit around it.

Morven volunteers to act as scribe.

"We would like to speak to the spirit of Alex Sanders," I say, my voice echoing in the rafters.

S O RL B DR

"We would like to talk to Alex Sanders," I repeat.

B O RREE

"Alex, are you there?"

CR T A H

At this point it is clear that we aren't getting anything, so we release the planchette. I am feeling very anxious and won-der if we will be successful.

"That wasn't him," Paul states. "It's just nonsense."
"Try again," Morven encourages.

"We only want to talk to Alex Sanders. Alex, are you there?" I ask.

YES

The planchette isn't moving in the way that I have come to understand as Alex. There is an odd feeling in the air. Still, I persist. "If this is you Alex, what do you have to say to us tonight?"

HEL O G RA T DHB L B R U

Raven says sternly, "Tell the two-year old to leave." "Is this the little boy who lives here?" I ask, referring to the child who haunts the hallways of the farmhouse.

EDWARD

"Edward, is that you?" Raven asks.

YES

"We'll contact you some other time. You have to go now." To my surprise, Raven speaks to the child's spirit in the firm, but loving, tone of a mother. The child responds with one last flourish of nonsense and then is gone.

We decide to try Alex again. "Alex, are you here?" I ask.

YES

"What do you have to say to us?"

A Voice in the Forest

K N O W L U V YES "

Alex, do you know anyone in this room?"

YES

"Do you know us all?"

NO

"Whom do you not know?"

HI N T

"Do you know Sulis?"

YES

"Do you know Ruanna?"

YES

"Alex, will you speak to us tonight?"

HI T A N I T H

Tanith looks up in surprise from the edge of the circle. She had spent some time with Alex when he was alive. "Long time no see, Alex."

G O DES L UVS U

"Oh, thank you, Alex!" Tanith beams.

HEL O T HN A S K

"You want us to ask you questions?" I say expectantly.

YES

The excitement in the circle begins to build. Morph calls out from across the room.

"Do you know me, Alex?"
To our surprise, Alex acknowledges his question by spelling out Morph's mundane name.

Alex then spells:
S UL I S

"Yes, Alex, I'm here," Sulis responds.

Out of the corner of my eye, I see Willow stir. Although she was given a message from Alex at Lammas, she has not yet had the opportunity of speaking with him directly.

"Do you know me?" Willow asks shyly.

KEEP T R UET O Y O RA R T

"Do you mean the Wiccan Craft?" she pursues.

NO

"Do you mean my work as an artist?" Willow is an accomplished illustrator.

YES

"Is there a piece of art you want me to do?" she asks.

A Voice in the Forest

W O MA N

"Any particular woman?"

G O DES

Willow smiles broadly and glances at me. The others be-gin to think of more questions.

"Anything for me, Alex?" Phoenix says.

DREA MS P EL

"I'll dream a spell?"

YES

"Alex, when I scry with fire, is that the salamanders' realm?"

MAYBE

"What can you tell Sulis about her group?" Morven asks. Sulis has been training students of her own for a few years now.

ELDRS

It is an appropriate response. Each of Sulis' three students has recently been elevated to the Alexandrian second degree. In our tradition they were now considered to be elders of the Craft.
"Any messages for Jack or me?" Raven asks quietly.

S T O P W O R R Y I N G

This elicits laughter from both Raven and Jack, so I assume Alex's comment makes sense to them.

"Any messages for me?" Morph is now wide-eyed and anxious. He, too, had only experienced Alex's first communication secondhand.

M A G I C I A N YES

We feel this is significant because Morph is very interested in ceremonial magick.

"Anything for me?" Ruanna asks.

O P EN HEA R T

"Anything for me Alex?" Paul whispers. I know he is getting tired, as am I. The planchette has been moving very energetically.

HA N DS

"Should I study holistic massage?" Paul's previous messages from Alex have been about the gift of healing.

YES W E L L

"To make others well?"

YES

"Anything for me, Alex?" I ask. I can feel the energy really beginning to wane now.

S T UDEN T S

"I know, Alex, you've had hundreds!" I laugh. "I hear you. I understand."
"Am I ever going to feel I'm competent to teach?" Morph asks.

A Voice in the Forest

YES

"When should I start?"

N O W G R O W

"Teaching others will make me grow?"

YES

"Are you serious about your rebirth in the year 2000?" Raven asks.

YES

"Do you have to, or do you choose to?"

L O N EL Y

"Will you be born to someone within our coven family?" Morven inquires.

NO

"Will it be in England?"

NO

"Will your mother be Wiccan?"

YES

"Will we know you again?"

I N T I ME

"Do you have anything else to say, Alex?" I realize that it must be very late.

Jimahl DiFiosa

We had cast the circle at the stroke of mid-night and the candles in the pumpkins have been out for a while now.

YES G R O W

Morven would later write: "At this time, Paul and
Jimahl break the communication, with Jimahl saying, 'Thank you, Alex.'"
Alex's presence hangs in the room for a long while. His words have rung as clearly in all of our hearts as if he had stood physically among us, as if he had embraced each of us. In a way he had, for he did not fail to come to us when we asked for him. And the words he spoke to each of us seemed, as they had before, to reach the core of our spirit.

I will remember the silence immediately after Paul and I let go of the planchette as being particularly noteworthy. We sit there on the floor of the carriage house, our robes drawn tight against the waxing chill. No one moves. I know we probably are each thinking the same thoughts, feeling the same mixed emotions — it is as if we were one soul, one mind.

That, in retrospect, is the magick of Alex Sanders.
When we do finally break the Circle and return to the farmhouse dining room to share our late night feast, there seems to be a renewed sense of hope in each of us. Samhain, after all, is the time of the year to acknowledge death not as an ending, but as another beginning.

Alex, deceased for ten years now, is still among us. He cares about us. He encourages us to grow and to become closer than ever before. He challenges us to live the Craft every day and to share the mysteries with new students. How perfect it all seems.
And so we end the evening by raising our glasses to him. "Hail to the King of the Witches," we sing out.

"Thank you, Alex," I whisper. "Thank you so much."

Jimahl DiFiosa

IV
Chapter Four

DREAMS AND QUESTIONS

A Voice in the Forest

Jimahl DiFiosa

It is nearly four in the morning when I lie down on an over- stuffed sofa in Raven and Jack's den to sleep, but sleep will not come easily. An antique clock somewhere in the house chimes on each half-hour and keeps me tossing from side to side. Like a boat without an anchor, my mind drifts randomly on an ebb and flow of consciousness, bringing thoughts and images of Alex to the forefront. Question after question surfaces — most of them impossible to answer.

How could he still be earthbound ten years after his death? Was he being hindered in some way from passing over? Was he communicating in this way with anyone else? Should we tell others about this? Would they believe us if we did? Could we just be imagining the whole thing?

Again and again the questions come rising up out of my half-asleep mind, and the clock in the other room keeps chiming. Eventually I resign myself to a sleepless night and position myself on the sofa to face a large window. Through the lace curtain I can see a slice of sky — already beginning to lighten with the dawn.

I awaken an hour or so later with bright light on my face.
It is still early and the rest of the house is quiet. I have been dreaming of Alex. Or rather remembering, in a dream colored with nostalgia, a vision I had of him shortly after his death:

It was the first of May 1988. Unknown to me at the time, Alex had passed away the day before. I was very new to the Craft then, having joined Morven's coven in early April. Morven had sent Alex news of the coven's formation. It was the last communication that they would have, and quite likely one of the final pieces of Craft news he would receive prior to his death.

A Voice in the Forest

I had gotten up just before dawn — which wasn't unusual for me — and gone into the living room of the suburban apartment where I lived at the time. I saw Alex Sanders standing in the center of the room. He was dressed in a white ceremonial robe. Having had some experience with lucid dreaming prior to this experience, I resolved that I was still asleep and made an effort to stay in the subconscious state as long as possible.

"Bring me your tools," Alex had said to me. I only had two magickal objects to call my own at that time. The first was my athame, the traditional double-edged knife used in witchcraft. The second was a blank book I had chosen as a future Book of Shadows. I would soon copy into it by hand all of the rituals and spells passed down to me by my teacher.

I did as he asked and brought the two humble items to him. Laying his hands on the book and the athame, Alex blessed them and encouraged me to be true to the Craft. He said that I would succeed with my studies and contribute significantly to the perpetuation of Alexandrian Wicca.

"Remember me," he said. "Leave a chair for me in all your circles. Tell the others."

Much later that day I received a call from Morven stating that Alex had died the day before. I hesitantly told her about my experience. I was self-conscious that she or the others might think it presumptuous of me to believe that the King of the Witches had visited me personally. Morven took the information to heart and, for many months thereafter, there was an empty chair next to the altar in every circle that we cast. It was understood that this chair was there for Alex if he should choose to visit our circle. But the chair eventually became much more than a token of remembrance — it became a symbol of our own commitment to the Craft.

The chair reminded us that since Alex Sanders was no longer incarnate, we were now responsible for keeping his tradition intact.

The chair became an icon for a sacred trust, one that weighed heavily on our hearts and minds, and — ultimately — one that would deeply influence each of our lives in the years ahead.

A noise above my head brings me back to the present. There is a creaky tread down the wooden staircase and Paul and Phoenix come into the room. Paul, too, has dreamed of Alex and is anxious to share his experience:

"I lay awake for a long time listening to the house settle around me. There are so many noises in an old house that you don't hear in an apartment building. Eventually I must have dozed off. I remember opening my eyes and seeing Alex standing over the bed. He was wearing the same white robe with the gold trim. He took my hand and brought me downstairs. I remember looking at myself and thinking that I shouldn't be wandering around someone else's house in my underwear. It was that real. We went into the living room. I saw you asleep on the sofa. Alex and I sat down in front of the fireplace and talked. There was a fire burning there — the room was very warm. I don't remember everything he told me, but one thing in particular stands out. He said that a great truth would be revealed to me in a dream. The sense of being face to face with him was very clear." Phoenix says that he was given a 'dream spell' during the night, exactly as Alex had mentioned in the previous spirit board session. It was a spell utilizing the element of fire. Being an extremely competent magician, Phoenix is especially adept at raising and directing 'dragon energy.'

The others are waking one by one and moving around in the rooms above our heads. We move into the chilly kitchen of the farmhouse and are delighted to see that Raven had set up the coffee service the night before. As the coffee brews, we sit around the kitchen table in fuzzy silence.

There seems to be a big question hanging over our heads

— like one of those balloons in a cartoon drawing. It is a question that none of us are prepared to answer: Now what do we do?

The smell of the coffee drifts through the house, summoning everyone to breakfast. Soon we are all participating in a lively discussion over a banquet of breakfast foods. I intentionally turn the subject to Alex.

Willow seems particularly disturbed and voices her concerns most pointedly. "I don't understand why he wants to reincarnate in the year 2000. We've just made contact with him. What's the hurry?"

"We still have more than a year," Morven reasons. "We'll use the time we have left wisely."

"But why do we have to race against the clock? It doesn't make sense. If this is Alex, he'd want to give us as much of his time as possible."

"Maybe it's not his fault that it took ten years for someone to make contact with him," I interject. "Imagine being around for a decade, standing in the background, just waiting." Willow persists, "But look at the statement he made about being lonely. How can he be lonely? There've got to be a lot of Wiccans on the other side."

"I don't think he's on the other side," I say flatly. "I think he's earthbound."

"Earthbound? You mean he never passed over? Never went anywhere? Just stepped out of his body and hung around?" Willow is clearly distraught. I understand why the subject of death causes her so much pain. A close relative who has been seriously ill for years is quickly losing ground. It would have been far more reassuring if Alex spoke of the afterlife as a land of enchantment and unending joy.

"Sort of like a ghost," Ruanna volunteers.

"Yes!" I say emphatically. "Exactly like a ghost."

"But why do spirits hang around?" Raven asks. "Do you suppose it could be unfinished business?"

"I don't know," I admit. "Perhaps it was a decision he made when he died. Maybe he wanted to stay around for a while. I remember reading a letter

he published just before he died. It said something like 'soon I will be with you all.' Maybe he
meant it literally."

"But ten years!" Willow shakes her head. "I don't get it."

This morning, over the bagels and cream cheese, there is clearly a nerve struck in our group soul that will resonate painfully over the months of winter's darkness that lay ahead. It is impossible for us to know at this time that we will never have the opportunity as a group to speak to Alex again. If we had known this, perhaps we would have shoved the junk food aside and brought out the spirit board one more time. Perhaps we would have spoken with Alex until all of our questions were answered. But within the group
there is a certain level of apathy that I find disconcerting. It is as if there is an elephant in the kitchen. And no one wants to acknowledge the elephant. This is Alex, King of the Witches. He has proven twice now that he is available to us. We can ask him anything. We can talk about the Craft and the Mysteries of the goddess. We can ask him the most intimate questions about his life. We can ask him why it was that he was compelled to remain between the worlds for over a decade — what pressing business did he leave unfinished?

But, instead, the conversation shifts to the weather, our children, and our plans for the winter holidays ahead.

After a while, we pack the cars and get ready to head home. I am quiet and Paul asks what is wrong.

"I understand why Alex is so lonely," I reply.

Jimahl DiFiosa

Chapter Five

DESCENT INTO WINTER

A Voice in the Forest

Jimahl DiFiosa

There was little contact with most of the others over the next few months. The days grew shorter and the nights longer. The cold weather came down like a curtain. As a pagan and a witch, I had grown accustomed to these seasonal tides. I understood that winter represented the season of darkness — a time when the inherent powers of growth and reanimation went underground. This was the time of the year for introspection, for quiet solitude, a cosmic opportunity for 'time out.' But this year the descent of winter also brought problems. I would later comment, when the world was again poised on the brink of spring, that the winter of 1998-99 had been the darkest I had ever known. I am sure this sentiment was also true for many of my immediate Wiccan family.

In retrospect, it became evident that the words Alex had spoken to each of us in the bright days of summer were prophetic in nature. If he spoke of learning laughter, it became evident that a heart-rending tragedy was looming on the horizon. If he spoke of the need for healing, it foreshadowed sickness and depression that would dominate the months ahead. If he admonished us to stay together, it foreshadowed a time when the bonds of our friendship would be tested beyond our comprehension. I reflected continually on the events of the previous months. Morven had meticulously transcribed each of the sessions and emailed them to everyone. I poured over the notes again and again looking for a clue as to Alex's expectations. There was a nagging feeling in my heart that preempted every other thought — Alex had more on his agenda than just stopping by to say hello on the way to the afterlife. There was something else he needed to say — something he needed to accomplish — and he was incapable of doing it alone.
At one point, I would write in my journal:

"If only there were adequate words to say exactly what it is that I want to say — perhaps if I could explain how heavily the thoughts of Alex weigh on my mind, the others would understand. There is not a moment that

A Voice in the Forest

I don't sense him waiting in the darkness — just out of reach — where he has likely been for years. The forest from which he first spoke to us has taken on a deeper meaning. No longer representative of only the campground in New Hampshire, the forest now must also be seen as a metaphor for the wilderness that lies between life and death. The wild place that Alex inhabits — described in his own words as 'lonely' — is the embodiment of all that humans dread. It is the great Unknown.

"No wonder we are disturbed by the idea of death. It is the one mystery that no man has solved. We can accept the business of living, for that is what we are good at — the calendar and the ticking clock are our best friends. We are carried forward from one life event to another. Our children are born and, as they grow, we see our youth reflected in their own. They immortalize us. They preserve us. The house and the yard and the seasons of life and death and rebirth as reflected in the wheel of the year are all manageable microcosms of loss and renewal. We can accept that the snow will fall and cover the earth only because we know that sooner or later the green will emerge again from the ice.

"But when a loved one looks at us for the last time, there are no words to describe how terrified we are. There are pictures out of books and stories that we tell each other about angels of light and the spirits of those who have gone before and who will welcome us over when our time comes. There are doctors who can wrap us in numb abeyance so that pain is a negligible side-effect. There is the faith of a thousand religions and the faces of a thousand Gods that all basically say the same thing — no one really knows! And whatever it is that we need to believe, we embrace.

"In the face of death, holding on to life is as natural as breathing. We resolve to face our end bravely when our time comes. We promise to be strong for those who depend on us for strength in crisis. But the bottom line is always the same: no one knows what happens in that final moment. I can understand, then, why a voice from the other side can inadvertently cause mixed emotions. To acknowledge that voice immediately takes us where we do not want to go. To hear that voice, we have to move beyond the world of the living and put ourselves in an unfamiliar space. This is a predictably frightening situation. And yet I see Alex in that forest every time I close my eyes. He is standing in the shadows, his face turned expectantly toward me. How deep are those woods, Alex? How far away have you gone to be so near?"

I will be the first to admit that I was becoming obsessed with Alex. I could not stop thinking about him. I was unable to relegate his few communications to the realm of happenstance. I sensed that there was work to do, mysteries to unravel, questions to be asked — and that somehow my personal involvement was necessary. A bond developed between Alex and me that defied explanation. If I closed my eyes, I saw him. When I slept, I dreamed of him. I resolved to do whatever I could do to help him. I promised him that I would take this as far as I could — that I would unselfishly give until there was nothing more I could give.

Morven listened patiently and agreed that there was more to the situation than we had originally thought. Always encouraging, always supportive, she urged me cautiously forward.
Paul and Phoenix spent hours with me — searching through old books and notes, scouring volumes of occult literature — looking for any mention of Alex Sanders.

Being a strong proponent of the 'power in numbers' theory, I also called two other Wiccan friends, Asha and Finbar, into service. Although they had been absent each of the previous times Alex had spoken, the personal messages that Alex sent to them had a profound impact on their lives.

"We would love to help," Asha said happily. "Anything you need, just let us know." And so it was that in the last vestiges of winter, our faces were turned once more toward the promise of light.
January went by quickly and Candlemas was once again upon us.

On February Eve, Paul, Phoenix, and Morven joined me in my Boston apartment to celebrate the sabbat.

The altar was adorned with white roses and shimmering mirrors. Tall white candles filled the room with fragile light. Encouraged by the inevitable greening of the year, I invoked the Goddess of Winter's End into our circle. "Between the snow and the equinox, we've many a road to wander."

When gods pass by, we hear their voice in rain and wind and thunder.

"But we're never alone as we make our way home, for green is the path that leads us.

"When dark and light meet as one, the Lady will be there to greet us!" At ritual's end we shared a feast of white food — delicate cakes shaped like crescent moons, slivers of almonds and a chalice of pale wine. We ate our ritual meal quickly because we were anxious to speak again with Alex.

The spirit board was then set up in the center of the small room. Morven took up a notebook and a pen and waited expectantly. Phoenix sat nearby with a digital camera. Paul and I sat down at the board and placed our hands on the familiar planchette. Dave, my partner at the time, was also present.

The room was still lit only by candles. One of them was brought from the altar and placed near the board so that we could better see its ornate letters. OK, Alex, you want to talk — we're listening. Let's go. And as sure as spring follows winter, the planchette jumped into motion.

Jimahl DiFiosa

Jimahl DiFiosa

Chapter Six

A LIGHT IN THE FOREST

A Voice in the Forest

Jimahl DiFiosa

The planchette moves quickly in erratic circles — covering the board again and again without stopping at any letters.
"We only want to speak with Alex Sanders," I state clearly. The planchette stops abruptly:

YES

"Alex, are we to understand this is you?"

MO R VEN

"Yes, Alex. I'm here," she responds. "Will you speak with us again?"

YES

"Did you see our ritual tonight?" I ask.

YES

"Do you know we think of you all the time?"

YES

There is a series of incomprehensible responses, followed by inactivity.

"Alex, is it difficult for you to communicate tonight?"

YES

"Why is that?"

I M F O G Y YES

"You're foggy tonight, Alex?"
"Why is that?"

YES

V E I L YES

"Maybe the veil is not that thin?" Phoenix suggests.

YES

"The veil is not thin between the worlds?"

YES D R I N K

"Is it because we've had something to drink tonight?" Morven asks.

NO

"Do you want something to drink?"

YES

"Where should we leave something for you to drink?"

WES T

Morven would later note: "We stop here to put some red wine in a glass and place it on a small table in the west. We know Alex prefers white, but we didn't want to stop long enough to open a bottle because we were afraid we'd lose him. At this point we also looked at the pictures Phoenix was taking with the digital camera. In the third one it looks like Alex's face is superimposed over Paul's face. As we're getting ready to restart, Paul notices small droplets of water on the planchette. There is no water nearby and no one is sweating!"

"Alex," Morven continues, "we gave you some wine."

YES

"Did you have some?"

YES

"Alex, was that you superimposed over Paul's face?" I ask.

YES

"Do you come into him physically when we do these sessions?" I pursue.

YES

"Always Paul?"

YES

"Then what is my purpose?"

M E D I U M YES

"I'm a medium? So, what is Paul?"

C HA N EL

"Paul is a channel?"

YES

"It takes two of us to contact you this way?"

YES

"Have I been a medium in a past life, Alex?"

YES

"Is it a talent I should I develop in this life?"

YES

"Alex, is there anything else you want to say to us tonight?" Morven asks.

S E N D B L E S I N G YES

"Alex, those blessings come from you?"

YES

"Is there anything you want us to do?"

C A RR Y O N

"Alex," I say, "we're doing that. Does this make you happy?"

YES

"Alex, do you know about Paul and Phoenix's new students?"

YES P R I E S T E S S E S

"Priestesses?" Paul remarks. He and Phoenix have recently begun to train three female students. Paul had commented to me previously that he sensed Alex's presence whenever they met with their students.

YES (and then another, more emphatic) YES

"Alex, am I a channel?" Paul asks.

YES

"Is this why I have health problems after these sessions?"

YES

"Can I control these problems?"

YES

"What should I do?"

WATER

"Drink it?"

YES

"Alex, do you have anything to say to Morven?"
He responds by spelling out her third degree name — a name he had chosen for her at the previous Samhain.
"You like my name, Alex?"

C O N G R A T S YES

"Do you have anything for me?" Phoenix asks.

D R A G O N S S U R O U N D U YES

"Anything for me tonight, Alex?" I wonder aloud.

S T U D E N T S

"Alex, is this the same message as the last time we spoke?"

YES

"Where will I find them?"

U W I L L F I N D YES

"I'm learning healing, Alex," Paul interjects.

YES

There was a sudden downshift in the energy.
"Alex, your energy wanes," I state. "Would more wine help?"

NO

"Is it time to go?"

YES

I immediately want more. In my mind I ask him to stay, to talk to us, to help us understand what it was that he needed.

I N T I ME

"In time?" I ask, surprised that he heard my mental question as clearly as the spoken ones.

YES

Morven would later write: "At this point Paul and Jimahl release the planchette, with Jimahl saying, 'He's gone.' Paul points out more droplets of water on the planchette, which quickly evaporate."

After the spirit board session, we review the digital images that Phoenix had taken. There is a series of shots taken with and without a flash in the candle lit room. One of them definitely shows a face — looking very much like a gaunt version of Alex — superimposed over Paul's features. Another photo shows a white beard-like substance projecting from my mouth, covering the chin area. I have a hunch we are looking at ectoplasm, and in the days ahead my research into the subject of spiritualism confirms this.

Ectoplasm, the books explained, is one of the most common symptoms of spirit manifestation. It often forms at the extremities or fingertips of a medium. The substance was described as a lucid pearl-like liquid which evaporates quickly. This had to be the substance we detected on the planchette. The books went on to explain that ectoplasm often appears to exit the mouth of the medium and fan out into the room as the spirit attempts to take physical form.

This evening is a breakthrough in many ways for me. I have some- how received a personal message from Alex. It is subliminal, but it rings through loud and clear. There is a shift in Alex's energy — a new sense of urgency is developing. I understand that what he wants is simply an opportunity to speak. Not just to me or to those of us who have crowded expectantly around the spirit board, but on a larger scale to any who would care to listen. The procreative impulse in humans eases the fear of death by assuring that we continue to live through our children. Perhaps Alex has to be reassured that he will continue to live through his Craft children.

Although a 'king' on his deathbed, Alex in reality left behind a fractured kingdom. I am left with unanswered questions. If he wants to speak to others, how can this be done? Is there enough time? Where should we go from here?

Morven, forever the most logical of us, states the obvious: "Ask Alex."

Jimahl DiFiosa

Chapter Seven

ASHA AND FINBAR MEET ALEX

A Voice in the Forest

Jimahl DiFiosa

The month of February went by quickly and the seasonal tides turned again. This time they brought the first hint of green to the city landscape. I had spent the last several weeks deep in research about mediums. I was intrigued by Alex's statements regarding the use of both a channel and a medium, as I had always thought the terms were synonymous. Interestingly enough, I learned that Alex was indeed correct. Although separate functions by definition, they are undeniably two ends of one thread in psychic operations. The mental picture that came to mind was that of a television or radio set-up. Bouncing unseen to us throughout the beautiful blue skies, across the mountains, through our living rooms and into our basements are uncountable waves and rays. The variation in their frequencies and sources is unfathomable and yet we can harness them, each for a different purpose. Each has a source — and each may have a destination. They have but to be snagged by our technologies and put to work for us.

The television antenna — before the days of satellite dishes and cable networks — could harness some of those waves. All of those with a certain wavelength got drawn in, traveling down the antenna's wires and into our sets. When my mother was a child, even the radio had a wire antenna to improve reception. She told me of the nights that the frayed wires were wrapped around a section of the frame of the box spring to improve reception from a small but powerful station a thousand miles away in the mountains of West Virginia. And she told me of the crackling and sparks that accompanied the music during electrical storms when her father used the box spring as an antenna! But all the antennas in the world would be next to worthless were it not for the technology that allows us to flip through channels or twist dials to fine-tune the waves that are attracted to our screens and speakers. An antenna is of little use without a tuner, just as a medium may be of little use without a channeler. The medium is akin to the antenna, pulling in large amounts of psychic current and funneling it through their own body into the room. Left unchecked, this energy can be extremely dangerous to the medium. And two antennas do not improve the reception!

The channeler, being at the other end of the psychic connection, then becomes the equivalent of the tuner. The signal is received, filtered and deciphered. Using this analogy, I was able to understand the tremendous roles that Paul and I played in our communication with Alex.

To prove or disprove this theory, we experimented with a variety of combinations in the channeler/medium roles. We found that Paul and Phoenix functioned well as a team, while Asha and I did not. It seemed as if our talents both leaned toward mediumship. Working as a team, we succeeded in drawing in a dizzying amount of energy, but we found it difficult to sort or to control.

By teaching me about mediumship, Alex also inadvertently helped me to understand one of the basic principles of magick. Polarity, often understood in the Craft to represent the balance of gender opposites, is not necessarily dependent upon gender at all. It is relative instead to the successful handling of magickal current in exactly the same manner as described in the antenna and tuner analogy. One person must be magnetic — drawing in the energy. But to utilize the incoming energy productively, another individual must become a reostat, a tuner — channeling the power in measured doses toward the desired goal.

Asha, Finbar, and I were invited to Paul and Phoenix's home for a Spring Equinox ritual. Joining us would be Paul and Phoenix's new students — three unique women whose physical appearance and personalities seemed to perfectly embody the three aspects of the goddess — maiden, mother, and crone.

Since Asha and Finbar had not been present at the previous spirit board sessions, Paul happily arranged for them to arrive a few hours before the students so that they could speak with Alex. We set up the spirit board in the ritual room and Paul and I assumed our usual positions. Asha, Finbar, and Phoenix sat nearby. Since most of this session was private, no notes were taken. I have tried to recreate the most significant dialogue.

Alex came through quickly and greeted us.

5 F O L DKI S B L ES EDB E

Asha and Finbar were overwhelmed. Although they had received individual messages from Alex at Lammas, the experience of having a private connection with him was very powerful. Asha asked most of the questions, seeking clarification of some difficult personal issues. Aside from the delay factor in having the planchette spell each word, it seemed as if Alex was seated next to us — every response to her complex questions proved to be insightful.
Asha had demonstrated, over the years I had known her, an inherent ability to transcend the physical and literally become a living vessel in which the goddess could manifest. Although all high priestesses are trained to perform this function to some degree, Asha consistently delivered far more than most. She surrendered herself unselfishly — instinctively tapping into the primal power of the goddess — and allowed that power to blow into a magick circle like a typhoon. One of my fondest memories of Asha channeling the goddess occurred about five years ago on a Maine mountaintop.

It was a rough period for me and I was faced with pressing personal problems. My life seemed like a worn thread that kept unraveling in the most inconvenient places. I had been backpacking with Asha and Finbar. We were all much younger at the time and, in retrospect, at the height of our physical endurance. Each of us shouldered heavy backpacks as we hiked up a hairline trail to the top of a moderate-sized mountain. We had started the ascent at midday and calculated more than enough time to reach the summit and set up our camp before dark. It would have been a realistic goal except for a streak of darkness that suddenly smeared the horizon — accompanied by the unmistakable rumble of thunder.

A Voice in the Forest

The storm came upon us quickly with all the usual bells and whistles. We were within a hundred yards of the top — scrambling over boulders the size of small houses — our feet resting precariously on ledges barely a foot wide. Miraculously we won the summit without injury and set about putting up our tent. In the downdrafts of the storm, the canvas billowed crazily. Asha took control of the situation, giving instructions to Finbar and me. We were barely successful in getting the tent staked down before the storm unleashed itself full throttle. The three of us huddled in the tent, in awe of the unpredictable power of nature.

As the thunder broke above my head, I was reminded of a private conversation I had shared with the goddess the day before. I had been sitting on the screened-in porch of their summer cottage and feeling very bad for myself. I had whispered to the goddess, "I've lost my fire. I am depleted. If you are still there for me, I need you to remind me of who you are. Show me the magick."

Tonight's storm passed quickly and when we went out into the cool clean air we found that the first stars of the summer evening were already ablaze in the indigo sky. We decided to improvise a ritual. Staring up into the arching canopy of space, both Finbar and I invoked the goddess into Asha. For a long while, there was silence. Then the sounds of the wind moved across the rocky summit and a voice, small and unfamiliar, came out of Asha. The voice formed syllables — sounds — nonsensical sounds and yet each murmur was packed with emotion. Eventually the syllables formed words and the words became a mantra that Asha chanted over and "Sun Moon Stars Planets Spinning Sky Earth, Sun Moon Stars Planets Spinning Sky Earth..."

To our delight, Asha was being gradually transformed. Her eyes blazed like molten stars and we realized that the goddess had answered our invocation and now stood before us. Unfortunately, she immediately had a problem with my attitude.

"How dare you tell me to show you the magick?!" came the unexpected

redress. I couldn't breathe. I stared into her eyes and felt suddenly like the most insignificant life form on the planet.
"Everything is magick. Look around you. You are the magick!"

Now, back at Paul and Phoenix's home, I was thinking that Asha has continued to be a clear vessel for the goddess throughout the years. She serves the Craft well in that regard. Unfortunately, whenever the goddess manifested through her, Asha was not able to benefit from the experience in the same wonderful way as those around her. Before the others arrived for ritual, she decided to ask Alex if there was a remedy to this situation.
"Alex," Asha asked, "when you gave me my message at Lammas it was just one word — goddess."

YES

"Alex, I understand that I have the gift of bringing the goddess through to her children. But I also need the touch of the goddess in my own life. How can I accomplish this?"

I L U V I S I S

It was an unexpected, yet appropriate, comment from Alex. Asha has always felt an affinity with Isis.
"Thank you, Alex. I do, too. Isis is a beautiful goddess."

YES

And then, in response to her questions, he spelled:

I N V O KET HN B A S K

"Bast?" Asha continued, "I don't understand."

NO B A S K

A Voice in the Forest

"Bask in the goddess energy that's been invoked, Alex?" I attempted to clarify.

YES

"I understand, Alex," Asha said, "but can other priestesses learn to do this?"

U T EACH THEM

"Alex, do you know our student?" Asha asked. She and Finbar were continuing the occult education of a young lady who had moved out-of-state shortly after her Alexandrian second degree elevation.

NO W O U L D L I K E TO

"I would like that, Alex. Do you have any advice on her training?"

B RI N G HER O N R O A DT O T HI RD

Asha and Finbar asked another series of complex personal questions and Alex continued to respond articulately. When all of their questions were answered, I turned the subject to other matters.
"Alex, it has been a difficult winter for many of our family. We are trying to follow your directive to keep everyone together and to grow. It hasn't been an easy task. Some of us in particular are facing difficult times. A few members of our family are having a crisis of faith. Do you have any words of advice?"

K E E P H E A D U P K E E P G O ING

"Alex, I've been getting the idea lately that there is something more you would like me to do with this information."

YES

"Is it your intention that this information be shared with people outside our immediate Wiccan family?"

YES T E L L T H E M

"How should I tell them, Alex?"

B OO K

"When should this book be written?"

S OO N

"Alex, tell them what?"

MA KEMA G I C K

Suddenly the planchette stood still in the center of the board. Finbar was smiling at me from the sofa. In an occult way, Finbar was perfectly matched with Asha. Whereas she exuded a primal, unapologetic current, akin to the element of water, Finbar's presence always contributed a stable, undeniably ancient energy. As quiet as a stone at times, the power that Finbar generated typified the element of earth — deep, well-anchored and as solid as a dolmen. "Looks like you're going to be writing a book," he said, laughing.

I called Morven when I got home later that afternoon to tell her the news.

"It doesn't surprise me," she joked. "Alex has never been afraid of publicity."

My head was spinning. Fortunately, I had planned to take a brief vacation from my mundane job. I would spend that time working on an outline for the project and reviewing all of the written information we had accumulated. One of the first items on my agenda was to tell the others who had been involved in the sessions of my intentions. I was aware that the story I was about to put on paper at Alex's request involved them all. It would not be an easy task to complete without communal support and encouragement.

"Like the Fool in the tarot deck," I wrote, "I have accepted the task that Alex has given me. I am stepping into the Void. Although I am terrified, I know this is what Alex wants me to do. I hope that each of you will embrace the project as I have. I would welcome any assistance or suggestions you might have." I emailed everyone concerned and waited for their responses.

Within days most of the votes were cast. There was enthusiasm from all of the expected sources — Morven, Asha, Finbar, Paul, and Phoenix. I felt general acceptance from most of the others; however, the greatest resistance to the project came from Willow. She was trying desperately to come to terms with her sister's recent death and was lost in her personal grief. Alex was understandably the last thing on her mind. She wished me well, but said she no longer felt enthusiastic about our efforts to communicate with Alex.

"Don't forget you promised him an image of the goddess," I reminded her.

"I won't have time to do that before he reincarnates," she said coldly. Her ambivalence about Alex had been apparent since All Hallows, and yet her decision not to complete the artwork for Alex puzzled me.

I sat on the project for several days, brooding over whether or not I should go forward. But I had made a commitment to Alex. I believed with all my heart that the spirit of this amazing man was still among us and that all he wanted was one last opportunity to speak. I could not let him down.

Jimahl DiFiosa

Jimahl DiFiosa

Chapter Eight

PROMISES TO KEEP

A Voice in the Forest

The small room is filled with my collection of occult art. Stony faces of gods and angels smile down on me from the walls. A small goddess altar over the desk holds an image of Diana, arms outstretched toward me, and a vase of daffodils from Asha's garden. Floor-to-ceiling bookshelves are filled to capacity with jars of herbs, hand-blended oils and incenses. On this rainy morning in late March, I have an experience that will dramatically change the scope of this project. I am at the computer in my study, trying to hash out an outline for the book. I had been thinking intently about Alex for several days. It occurs to me that if I place myself in a light trance, perhaps the writing will come more easily. At least I could filter out most of the irrelevant thoughts and focus solely on Alex. I am not the greatest when it comes to trance work, so it takes a bit of effort. Eventually though, I am able to alter my breathing enough to encourage a relaxed state of mind. It seems to be helping immeasurably with my memory recall.

Suddenly I sense Alex very close to me, as if he is physically standing behind me. I sense that he wants me to purify myself with salt and water. I push the notion out of my mind and continue writing. I am not in a ritual mind-set and the idea of using water around a computer seems naturally unwise. But the impulse to purify grows stronger. I give into it after a few minutes and go to the kitchen to get a bowl of water and some salt. Returning to the study, I place the elements on the edge of the goddess altar and consecrate them with my index finger. I then light a stick of incense. There is a framed photo of Alex on the wall. I take it down and place it next to me, on the desk. I sit down again and try to resume work. Alex's presence is again very strong just behind me. I am dressed casually in my sweats — typical clothing for a day home from the office — but I begin to feel that my wardrobe is inappropriate. "Put on a consecrated garment," he seems to be saying. At this point I want to see where all of these preparations are headed — so I get up, strip off the sweats and slip into a ritual robe. If I have to go through this every time I work on this

project, it will take years to complete it!
Again, I sit down at the computer keyboard to resume work. Al- most immediately, I feel a strange sensation on my back and neck.

It is as if some essence of Alex passes effortlessly through me from behind. My hands are suddenly moving all over the keyboard. I type rapidly. When I finish a moment or two later, I am shaking. I am amazed to read the result. It is typed all in lower case with many misspellings and typos, so I edit the text to make it readable.

I am Alex Sanders, King of the Witches. It has been a long time since I wrote, spoke, moved about in the physical world. Many of you have no doubt forgotten me. Some have not. I would hope that you are in remembrance of me, but I was a man and men die all the time.

It is dark here. There is no light. A kind of purgatory, I suppose, if you think of the afterlife as a waiting room of sorts. I could have reincarnated long ago, but I chose to remain earthbound. So I am caught between the worlds.

I drift like smoke about you. I inhabit your rooms, your sacred spaces. My spirit goes to the circles where I am welcome. I observe. I watch. I try to teach but it is difficult unless those incarnate are receptive. For who can listen to the words of a spirit? Not a man who can stand up and be counted as one to hear, but a spirit of a man once known as King of the Witches. Even now there is rancor among you. There is division. There is doubt that I can exist in this way and in this time, but the irony is that this is the natural order of things. I can do what I wish. I have attained that power in many past lives. I am what I say I am, King of the Witches, and abeyance is due me. If not for any other reason but that I am the forefather of who you are. And as I now am, so you will be and your children's children shall look after you as you look after me. And so the Craft goes on, it never dies. It never stops. It can't — you must see to that. I could care less if you use my name 100 years from now, but the goddess must have her due worship.

I am Alex Sanders, of that there is no doubt. I want to talk about the goddess. And the Craft of the goddess — that which is and always has been and that which will continue for ages to come. I want to teach you what I could not teach you in my lifetime. I want to show you the way of all true magick.

There is a great circle of life and of being that encompasses all humanity. I can see it from here. We are connected on every level. You often make the mistake in perception to think that your lives begin and end at the end of your own existence. Imagine yourself as the centerpiece of a great wheel. You seem complete in your self. You can turn and move in any direction. You are a circle and your hands, the tips of your fingers, the toes on your feet all touch the perimeter of the circle. But there is so much more.

I will leave you now. We'll start again another time. Be in peace and goddess rest.

I don't know what to think. I am seriously worried that I have just lost my mind. I stare at the words on the computer screen until the screen-saver kicks on, startling me. I laugh nervously and resolve to get some fresh air. Before powering down, I email Morven and Paul — attaching the day's message.
"I don't know what to make of this. Let me know your thoughts," I write.

It is three days later and the silence of the others has become unnerving. Neither of them responds to the email. I am wondering if they figure I've gone into the deep end of the pool and are just being too polite to say anything. If you can't say anything nice, don't say anything at all. In retrospect, I understand that the isolation and anxiety I was experiencing was a direct result of a deep empathy I had established with Alex. I had foolishly convinced myself that I was suddenly left alone with this project. I again anguish over Willow's disinterest and I worry that I am just imagining the whole thing. The idea that I am making a fool out of myself seems a real possibility. Nevertheless, my commitment to Alex weighs heavily and I sit down again at the computer to put words to page.

A Voice in the Forest

Suddenly, I sense myself entering into a trance deeper than I've ever felt before. It is quite involuntary on my part — I can't seem to stop it from happening so I just let go.

It feels as if I am floating just outside of my body. Again there is a flurry of activity at the keyboard. It is over in just a few minutes. When I read what I have typed, I start to cry. I realize, for better or worse, that I am married to this project.

I am Alex Sanders, King of the Witches. I come to you from across the eons. I watch the fire of the sun illuminate a fertile land. I see how difficult it is for those who follow the old ways to see the path that will lead them forward, to recognize the dangers that lie before them. I understand how hard it is for those who love the goddess to keep a clear mind and unfettered will so that they can be about her business without interference from those who would declaim her virtues and deny even the most basic rights to those who follow her. This is a strange, new world. I find myself inside it as an archetype. I am out of my element. Around me there are faces I do not know and when I seek for those who knew me as a man, there is only silence. There is no reply to my inquiry. I am alone and this is a very dry place for me. I will move on soon, as I do not see the need for me to remain earthbound much longer. How quickly they turned to the memory of me, but once the time moves by and they forget, then the memory of me fades quickly, like a flower. I am forgotten of many, no longer the King of the Witches, and this causes me much consternation.

I see that there is a thread, a river of red life that still flows and it is to this river I am drawn like a moth to the fire. And when I see that there is a circle of elders still following the path I made, I am glad. My spirit rejoices. I understand how important it was to wait until I move on. I see that this has not been in vain. You ask me what I would have you do — I would have you tell the others that magick is real. Witchcraft is real. I devoted my life to it. I saw the age of the goddess dawn over mankind.

I came to the Craft in a time when speaking her name was dangerous.

I came to her when the dark of the moon was the only time we could worship her for fear of discovery, when the living room became the temple of Isis and the basement, dark and secret, became the place for our library. How we hungered for our freedom then, how we dreamed of a time when we might utter the secret name of the goddess in public without consequence. All of this has come about in a short period of time and even now the cult of the goddess grows. It grows from the dead wood of Christianity, for there are those who see the mother of god as the creatress [sic] and wonder aloud why she has been allowed to squander her power in the shadow of a sacrificial son. I see that she is once again in the forefront of a religion that will continue to progress as the years ahead unfold and this is a sign that the way of the goddess will become more palatable to those who seek her.

I see that the ways of magick are no longer hidden and you may find the secrets of the ages on any bookshelf in any store. They are so accessible that the reverse danger is evident that there is a tendency to take all things for granted, to see them as common things that have no weight. This is a trap of the mind and must be avoided. The mysteries of the goddess are stronger and deeper than time. They defy time. And I can see that now more than ever they become visible to any one who looks with their eyes. As a path in the forest, they beckon and the true seeker has no alternative but to follow. These are amazing times and the keepers of the mysteries must be aware of how critical it is to keep true to the path and to make the way smooth for those who will follow their footsteps.

More than ever before man looks for an answer to questions asked for thousands of years. The secrets of space are open to us. The secrets of the earth are open to us. The secrets of the universe are open to us. How then can any true seeker of the Craft be denied? How then can any true witch, or one that calls himself a hidden child of the goddess, say there is no magick? For magick is in the word, the spoken word. Magick is in the breath of every child and in the love of the mother for the child — how then can we be sad? How then can we be dismal? Wake up the heart that slumbers and look to the dawn of a new day for it is a glorious dawn. I come to you now as a teacher and entrust you with these words.

As fantastic as it seems to you, you must be brave enough to pass them on to any who will listen. You must allow me the opportunity to speak once more before all is changed — before the end of the Eon. For there has never been a better time to look at the facts as they are.

I devoted my life to the goddess, but as a man I made many mistakes. That is the mortal way and unavoidable to the most ingenious of us. I pissed people off, to say it bluntly. I turned them against me, particularly at the end when there was no place for me to go but down and it seemed as if they all waited for it outside my door. Like wolves they waited and when the king was dead they wailed like children. How sad I am that I did not have more time, or the knowledge that eluded me all those years. I hungered for a touch of the goddess and she came to me again and again and still I wanted more. I deserved it, I told myself. She owed it to me.

The goddess, as we see her, is so small. She is just a piece of our mortal fancies and we envision her in manageable portions. Like a piece of meat upon our plates, we cut her up and examine her and when we swallow we want to be certain we don't choke ourselves with her. So she becomes small and insignificant. We dress her and adorn her with memories of past lives and we awaken within ourselves the threads of memory that allow us to see her in a way that does not consume us. But when we awaken any aspect of the true goddess, we awaken the great beast of the goddess that has no safety valve attached. We can't deflate her by pulling a cork. She is big, beyond any reasoning — beyond any imagining — and a true invocation of the goddess takes one into the Abyss. We must be prepared to experience all of her, not just the parts of her that we are comfortable with. She is a beautiful goddess — but she is all that is and was and will be. The earth is the body of the goddess and the earth moves and shakes and shudders beneath us. The earth can heal and it also destroys. It swallows us whole without apology and begs for more. So the primordial goddess is more than we can envision and the words of a priest of the goddess must be chosen carefully for this reason. I honor her. I adore her. And there is no reason for me not to endorse her to you, for the way of the goddess is the path of truth. Go to her then and be absorbed by her — even when she breaks you down, you will profit in the end.

There are many that profess to know her and who speak the way of magick. Perhaps they read the books and memorize what it is that they feel they should know — but they do not know her. Their lives are devoid of her. They are limited by fears that manage their lives. This fear dictates what they will never become and when it comes time for them to exercise will over matter they cannot do so. They are slaves to matter. Their will is undeveloped, and that is a danger to them.

Know then that many are called but few are chosen. Even among your own, you can see those that have come to the goddess untruthfully. They stand on ground that is not solid. Even among your own you must recognize those who are the old souls who have walked this path before. Magick then is serious business. You cannot fool with it without consequence. Mind my words lest you destroy yourself with your own pride. That is the first lesson I would leave you. Be true to your Craft and do not give your word lightly. You must be prepared to back up your word with your life, and the goddess may very well demand such allegiance one day. Why then have I come now to speak this way through you? The answer is simple — you are willing to allow me to move through you. I will use you by your own invitation to say what I will say. And then I will walk away. You ask what it is I want to say and I shall reveal it to you in time. It has been a long while since I had a voice. I must pace myself and, for your safety, I will proceed with caution.

When Morven and Paul receive the second email, the response is immediate.

"Wow!" Paul says eloquently.

Morven, although moved by Alex's words, urges me to be cautious. "Channeling in this way can lack credibility. Traditional methods of divination are much more believable. I don't doubt that this is from Alex, but you are a very intelligent, articulate person and some people may think that the words are coming not from Alex, but from your own subconscious. My concern is that if you lose credibility in the reader's eyes, Alex loses credibility as well."

"I understand," I say, "but the end justifies the means. He wants to speak and by comparison the spirit board is so laborious. I am feeling a new sense of urgency to gather as much information as possible"

"Stay focused, Jimahl," she encourages. "It will all come together. This is a tremendously important work."
Still feeling shaky about Alex's direct communication with me, I send the messages to Asha. She calls me a few nights later and reads them back to me on the phone. It provides an interesting perspective and it is as if I am hearing Alex's words for the first time. When she finishes, there is a long period of silence before she speaks again.

"I can hear Alex in these words. It is as if he is speaking them aloud."

"I don't know what to do, Asha. Do I include them in the book?"

"How can there be a question?"

"But what will people think?"

"Your ego has no place in this project, Jimahl. None. Remember the promise you made to Alex. You have never broken a promise before. You can't break this one."

"I have to be realistic, Asha. I don't know if I can do this. It's too much."

"Jimahl, you are so fertile right now. You are like a root that has lain dormant in the earth for centuries, and from that root new life stirs. There is fresh growth inching its way toward daylight. If you give up now, the root will die. Nourish the plant, give it light. Once it breaks the surface, the green will keep on growing. Trust me. You have no idea how important it is for you to complete this project."

She ends the conversation shortly afterward and promises to visit in the near future.

"I bought a new spirit board," she says. "I'd like to take it for a test drive."

Jimahl DiFiosa

☿
Chapter Nine

ASHA AND JIMAHL CONTACT ALEX

A Voice in the Forest

Asha, true to her word, stops by for dinner a few nights later. Finbar is delayed at the office and promises to be along shortly. Dave is always happy to see Asha, as they are both artists. This commonality between them has created a special friendship that provides endless opportunities for conversation.

After some lively discussion, Dave excuses himself to work on dinner. Asha suggests we try her new spirit board. As an experiment, we join hands over the board before beginning and recite a traditional incantation, making a clockwise stirring motion above the planchette. It seems to raise a lot of energy and when we place our hands on the planchette, we find that it immediately starts to circle the board rapidly. Around and around it goes. Our fingertips are barely able to keep up with the momentum.

We both laugh, realizing that the planchette is obviously riding the unseen field of energy raised by our invocation. I remember Alex's words from the last channeling session: Magick is in the word, the spoken word. How incredibly clear the art of invocation suddenly becomes to me. Every word we speak has the potential to become a spell, an invocation. If magick is in the word, and if the power of the spoken word creates currents as tangible as this — then the heart and mind of a magician must be forever in control of what is said and thought. Eventually the movement slows and we are able to gain control of the planchette.

"Alex," Asha intones, "we want to speak with you. I read the words that you gave to Jimahl. We are part of that red river you speak of — that thread of life that keeps the Craft alive. Speak to us Alex, King of the Witches."

The response is immediate.

A Voice in the Forest

WI T HY O U

"Is this Alex Sanders?" she asks.

B L ES S EDB E

"Alex, this is the first time that Jimahl and I have worked together on the spirit board. Is it OK with you that we communicate as a team?"

YES B R E V I T Y

"You're asking us to be brief in our questions?"

YES

"Alex, Jimahl has shared the two messages he received. These are incredible communications."

C HA N N EL G

"Alex, were you channeling them through Jimahl?"

YES

"Alex, is it better to use the spirit board in this way to speak with you? Or do you prefer channeling as a method?"

A NY

"Any method is fine?"

YES

There is a lull in communication at this point. After a few moments of silence, I ask if Alex is still there. There is no response.

Finbar comes in shortly afterward and we decide to try again. He agrees to take notes.

There is a lot of confusion this time. The planchette moves erratically, first going to yes and then goodbye — over and over.

"Alex," Asha calls out loudly, "speak with us again. King of the Witches, answer our call."

The air seems thick with energy. The planchette continues to move in a moronic way. I realize that Asha and I are moving vast amounts of energy but none of it is making any sense.
"We're both mediums. We need a channeler to control the influx of astral data. If we keep going at this rate we are going to blow a circuit or two," I warn Asha.

"Let's try harder," she insists. "Focus, Jimahl. We can do this."
It is much more difficult than working with Paul. My head is throbbing. I feel like a motor on overload, but I finally resolve to allow Asha to draw the energy into the room and resign myself to becoming its conduit. We are like two dancers, both trying to lead. I relax the controls, and let Asha sweep me effortlessly across the dance floor.

Eventually the planchette starts to spell real words and a fresh connection with Alex is established.

MA KEMA G I C KMA KEMA G I C K

The planchette spells the same phrase over and over. There is a sense of immediacy in the message. "We are the keepers of the mysteries, Alex. We are making the magick." Asha is now speaking in a trance voice. Waves of energy wash over her and fill the room.

YES B L E S S I N G S

A Voice in the Forest

"Blessings to you as well, Alex. What do you have to say to us tonight?" Asha's trance voice is startling. Dave pokes his head into the room and gives me a quizzical look.

B E T R UET O W O RK

"Is this the book you are referring to, Alex?" I ask.

YES B E T R U E T O O T H E R S

"Do you like what I've done so far?" I had been feeling very proud of the fact that I had finally finished the first chapter.

B A REB EG I N N I N G

My heart sinks. "Is there anything you can say to help me, Alex? This is very difficult."

A S KHP S

"Ask a High Priestess for help?"

MO R VEN

"Is there anything else, Alex? Any others words of en- couragement?" The temperature in the room has climbed. My throat is dry. Finbar is scribbling wildly, a tense look on his face. Asha remains tightly in control of the moment.

P ERS EVERE

"I'll try, Alex. I'll do my best."

Y O U N O W M U S T E D U C A T E OT H E R S

Jimahl DiFiosa

"Will you help me?"

YES B E L I E V E

"How much time do we have, Alex?" I have a feeling that the stakes are much higher than originally anticipated.

U KN O W

"Alex, I don't sense there is as much time as we originally thought. How much time do we have? Please just answer the question."

EI G HT

"Eight what, Alex? Eight months?" I calculate quickly. It is now April 1999. Eight months will take us into the year 2000. It must be eight months.

"Alex," I continue, "is there anything else we need to know?"
There is no response. The energy starts to wane quickly. Asha lets go of the planchette with a great sigh and slumps in her seat. It takes her a moment to come out of the trance. I am trembling, breathing hard. My shirt is soaked with perspiration. I look up at Finbar, still writing feverishly on the pad of paper.
Dave walks into the room carrying a platter of roasted turkey with all the trimmings. "All righty, then," he says. "I think I need a cigarette after that! Anybody hungry?"

After dinner, Asha volunteers to help me with the dishes. She is standing at the kitchen window admiring a terra-cotta pot of fragrant rosemary.

"Rosemary for remembrance," she says softly. I think of Willow and silently send her strength.
v
"Any thoughts on tonight's session?" I ask.

"Be true to the story and the others. But above all, believe," Asha summarizes. "It all makes perfect sense." "Easy for you to say," I reply as I toss her a dish towel.

Jimahl DiFiosa

Chapter Ten

DARK WATER

A Voice in the Forest

In the early weeks of April, the thread of communication that we had so diligently guarded starts to unravel. It begins with Asha's curious dream.

She sees herself in a boat — it is night and the water that moves the boat forward is as black as the starless sky. The boat is old and in need of repair. The dark water seeps in through cracks in the hull. There is an oar missing which makes it impossible to navigate the craft. So Asha resigns herself to the will of the sea. The boat lurches forward on an unseen tide, eventually coming to rest on the shore of a deserted beach. A house can be seen further inland and Asha gets out of the boat and moves toward it. Sounds of friendly conversation can be heard drifting from the house. Asha sees the inhabitants of the brightly lit rooms through the open windows. It seems as if a celebration is in progress.

Asha is on the porch now. She steps into the warmth of the house. There is a sudden silence — all heads turn in her direction. She is clearly a stranger in this place.

"I'm looking for Alex Sanders," she stammers.

There is a murmur of acknowledgment and someone directs her to the garden in the rear of the house. Asha goes outside into the backyard. The air is thick with the scent of flowers, their perfume heavy on the breeze. She finds Alex walking there with a matronly woman on his arm. Asha greets Alex warmly but is surprised to learn that Alex does not know her. "I'm one of Morven's students, Alex. You've met Morven. Do you remember her?"
Alex again shakes his head. He then extends his hand to Asha and introduces her to the woman at his side, whom he identifies as his mother. Asha called me the day after the dream and was clearly disturbed.

"It doesn't make sense that he didn't know you," I reassure her. "You just spoke with him last weekend."

As she related the dream to me, I also became concerned. The leaking boat, the seething water, the mysterious house on a lonely island — all of it seemed loaded with dark imagery.

My own dream came a few nights later. Many of the elements were the same....

I am walking at night along the bank of a river. Suddenly a dark wave rises out of the water, surges over the bank and sweeps me off my feet. I am thrown into an unrelenting current and am powerless to resist.

The momentum of the water carries me forward and leaves me stranded on a strange shore. There is a house in the distance — the light from its windows blazes invitingly. I enter the house, just as Asha did, but in my dream no one turns to acknowledge my presence. I ask about Alex. But no one hears me. I start moving through the festive crowd — looking for Alex.

They speak to each other fondly — this is obviously a reunion of old friends. But no one seems to notice me. Alex is nowhere to be found....
'Very interesting,' Paul comments when I tell him about the two dreams. "Have you been able to sense Alex around lately?"
"No. I can't make contact with him no matter how hard I try."
"Perhaps we should try the spirit board together one more time?"
"Thank you," I say. "If we could speak with Alex again — even briefly — he may be able to tell us what is going on."

A few hours later we are huddled over the familiar board. Paul and I are on the planchette. A link is established quickly but it is very weak. Alex spells out Morven's third degree name — it has become a means of identification between us. Paul and I make a concerted effort to sustain the connection, but there is a definite strain. It seems as if we are playing an astral game of tug-of-war and the other team is pulling harder on the rope than we are. The plancette moves slowly — creeping across the board like the dark water in my dream.

"Alex, can you speak with us today?" I ask hopefully. The response is quick and decisive.

NO

"No? Alex, you've never said 'no' before." I am shocked by his negative response. "Please, Alex, just a few questions…"
There is a moment's hesitation and then:

TRY

"Alex, what is happening on the dreamscape? Can you explain the meaning of these dreams?"

PARANORMAL

"Alex, where are you right now? Why is it so difficult to speak with you?"

SEA OF BLACKNESS

"Alex, there seems to be tremendous opposition to our communication today."

WOMAN

"Alex, is it a woman who is making it difficult to speak with you? Who is this woman?"

DESOLATION

The planchette creaks to a sudden halt. "Alex, are you still there? Alex?"

A Voice in the Forest

There is no response. I look at Paul. His face is as long as mine.

"Alex, please talk to us," I insist. "Tell us what to do. Give us some direction on how to proceed. Alex...?"

"It's best to let him go for now." Phoenix says. "He either doesn't want to answer your questions or can't."

"Can't? What's that supposed to mean?"

"I don't know, Jimahl. I don't have any answers."

For a short while we brainstorm about the possibility of potential adversity to the project. It doesn't make sense that anyone would make an intentional occult effort to sabotage our efforts. We go around and around the ring of possibilities until we are exhausted. It seems obvious that we are muddying the water even more in our attempt to see clearly. So we all agree to walk away from it for a few weeks.

Beltane is nearly upon us. The second of Paul and Phoenix's students is scheduled to take her Alexandrian first degree on May 2nd. They have a lot of preparations to make. I am cognizant of the tremendous amount of physical and mental time this project demands from my friends.

And, personally, I am exhausted. "We'll reconvene after Beltane," Paul says encouragingly. "Perhaps we all just need to take a break."
Asha calls with interesting news a few days later. "I just realized that April 30 will be the eleventh anniversary of Alex's death."
I look at the lunar calendar tacked up next to the phone, and I smile.

"And there will be a bright full moon that night. I hope Alex enjoys it."

Jimahl DiFiosa

A Voice in the Forest

2007 - Morven, Paul and Jimahl in one of the last communications together with Alex Sanders

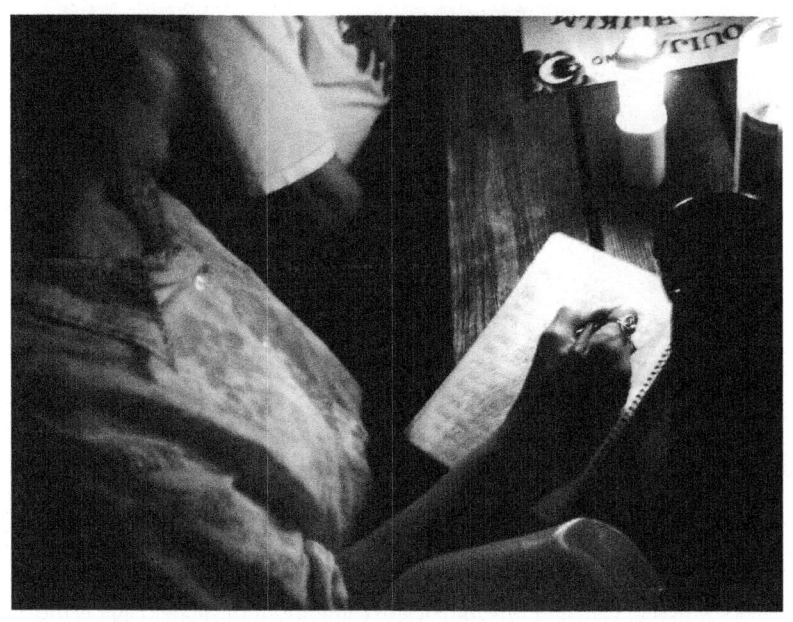

2007 - Morven takes notes on the session as the letters are found in the board

A Voice in the Forest

2007 - Reading of the notes after the session

1998 - Morven, Paul and Jimahl (back to camera). In the upper right is the impromptu altar with its glass of wine for Alex, as described in Chapter Six.

Jimahl DiFiosa

1998 - Jimahl, Paul and Morven (back to camera).

2007 - An altar in the Forest

A Voice in the Forest

Paul and Jimahl attempt to contact Alex by using the spirit board. When this photograph was examined closely, shadows were visible around Jimahl's mouth and fingertips, and thought to be ectoplasm.

The lake, at the Campground, New Hampshire, USA, 2007

Jimahl DiFiosa

New Hampshire, 2007 - The forest of "A Voice in the Forest"

New Hampshire, USA, 2007 - The morning mist at the Campground

A Voice in the Forest

2007 - Morning time in the Campground. Karagan, in his cape, walks across the morning mist at the Campground

New Hampshire 2007 - At night, after all is done, the witches gather around the fire

Jimahl DiFiosa

The informal Alex Sanders, relaxing at his Sussex, England at home in 1986

Alex chatted freely about many things with his visitors from "across the pond," and posed for informal shots in his sitting room. He frequently entertained visitors from all over the world.

This is the Alex that Lady Morven recalled, the reflective founder of the tradition of Wicca that bears his name — a wise and sometimes solitary man who had not lost his wry sense of humor.

Alex posed for his visitors in his magickal regalia.

The Magickal Alex Sanders, 'King of the Witches' 1986
here is a weariness in Alex's eyes that belies the illness that plagued his final days, but a strong sense of self and purpose still emanates from him.

Fondly examined the items on his personal altar, having placed a bouquet of deep blue-violet iris to honor his beloved Goddess.

From let to right: Phoenix, Jimahl and Paul 2004

Jimahl DiFiosa

Jimahl DiFiosa

Chapter Eleven

THE FINAL COMMUNICATION

A Voice in the Forest

Paul is the one who eventually places the missing piece into our communal puzzle. On May Eve he had a dream about Alex that pulled the out-of-focus picture into clearer perspective.

"I saw 'Alex in Summerland,'" he tells me excitedly. "It was a huge Beltane celebration. He was very happy — finally he is with other Craft people who have passed on. There are a lot of other witches there. Alex is not lonely any more. He's gone home."
"But what about the dreams Asha and I had?"

"Perhaps the dreams were a premonition that Alex was about to make the transition into Summerland. The dark water in the dreams could have represented the space that divides the world of the living from the world of the dead. There are many multi-cultural references to this void as a body of water — the River Styx, for example." "A sea of blackness?" I interject, remembering Alex's words. "Exactly, and although rest, renewal and regeneration await the soul after the journey, the trip across that water has got to be scary. Perhaps the woman Alex called 'desolation' is the dark aspect of the goddess — the watcher between the worlds, the Queen of the Underworld." "There's still the unsettling fact that Alex did not recognize Asha in her dream."

"I've been thinking about that." Paul says thoughtfully. "You told me at Samhain that you were positive Alex was still earthbound. Do you remember?"

"Yes, his connection with us was so strong."

"This is just hypothetical," Paul explains, "but perhaps when the soul passes over to the other side it sheds the trappings of the mundane self. The sacrifice of remembrance may be a part of that process."

A Voice in the Forest

I take a moment and reflect on Paul's conjectures. As much as I want to embrace them, I still find myself resisting the idea that Alex has moved on so quickly.

"He said he would reincarnate in the year 2000," I say stubbornly.

"This is only May 1999."

"Jimahl," Paul laughs, "when was the last time you studied biology? The human gestation period is nine months. Do the math. After all, he never said when in the year 2000."

For several days I think about my conversation with Paul. Then one afternoon when I am home alone I feel the familiar rush of energy that I have come to associate with Alex.

It is as if an astral phone is ringing. I sink down effortlessly into a deep trance and a brief flash of communication comes through me. It occurs in the same manner as the previous channeling sessions. Afterward, I stare at the words on the computer screen for a long while and then silently resolve to keep this information from the others.

Perhaps I am playing a psychological game with myself. I believe the message is not only genuine but of tremendous importance. But it also provides closure to these remarkable events. I simply do not want to accept this. I want to believe that the temporary lull in our communication with Alex will end soon. I want to believe that Alex's voice will come again in the greening of the year and that he will continue to enchant and inspire us with his wisdom. But in my heart I know Paul is right. I remember my joke to Asha about hoping Alex enjoys the full moon. Alex had enjoyed the full moon on the eleventh anniversary of his death. The light of that moon was enough to lead him out of my metaphorical forest and across the dark water that separates the worlds.

I print one copy of Alex's final communication and delete the file from my hard drive.

Jimahl DiFiosa

♂
Chapter Twelve

THE GREEN THAT KEEPS ON GROWING

A Voice in the Forest

Jimahl DiFiosa

The first of May turns out to be one of those rare spring days when it seems as if all of nature is exhaling. Everything smells of blossoming trees and green grass and freshly turned earth. The sky is storybook blue. There is not a cloud in sight.

I have been invited to spend the afternoon at Raven and Jack's covenstead. The windows of the old house are thrown open and the smell of summer's awakening fills the rooms.

Sulis and Ruanna are at the table, weaving flowers from Raven's garden into a crown for the maypole. Their faces are radiant. I look at them — really look at them — and it is as if I am seeing each of them for the very first time. The sun paints patterns in Ruanna's auburn hair. Her hands work steadily at the crown — each delicate bloom weaves between her fingers and is absorbed miraculously into a tapestry of glorious color. Sulis sings softly as they work. It is an old song, a song of hope renewed and the turning of the wheel from dark to light.

Jack and Morph are in the garden, placing a tall, neatly trimmed fir tree into a freshly dug hole. Raven runs to meet them. Her long hair is woven with flowers. She ties red and white ribbons to the top of the pole. The door to the house slams and Sulis runs down the gar¬den path with the flower crown. Her bare feet tap hollow music on the warm earth. "Wait!" she calls out. "This is for the top of the pole. Wait for me!"

Standing at the edge of the garden, I watch as the maypole is set into place and secured. The wind takes Raven's red and white ribbons and teases them into a tempest.

Morven comes up behind me. "The Craft is a living thing," she says quietly. "It will never die."

I put my arm around her and pull her closer. "I hope Alex is smiling on us today."

"I'm sure he is," she replies, her face turned toward the golden light of the sun. "He must be very proud of all of us."

We dance the maypole into existence, weaving our ribbons tighter and tighter. As we spin happily around the tall tree, a flash of images rolls across my mind. Each mental photo hangs vividly in the space above our heads. I remember the first time I set foot into a ritual circle, the smell of the incense, the warmth of the candles near my skin. I remember Willow standing beside me, watching breathlessly as Morven opened the Book of Shadows and began to read the ancient words of power for the first time. I see all of us in the forest — huddling around the campfire as we raise paper cups of wine to the gods. I taste again every crescent cake ever blessed at
circle's end. And I remember in a dizzying, heart-rushing moment every second of elation we felt together, the exhilaration and power of our rituals, and conversely the inevitable moments of confusion and pain when one of us faltered.

How strong our hearts still beat. And the ribbons are wound tighter still. How alive we are. And the red and white ribbons at last become a finished work of art, a tangible reminder of how succinctly each of our lives are woven into and around the lives of the others. When we are finished, a fat rabbit ambles across the green grass. It seems to be an acceptable omen for our future.

On the second of May I am invited to Paul and Phoenix's covenstead to witness a first degree initiation. This is the second of their students to be initiated within the past few months. It is a beautiful ritual, austere in the ways that initiations must be — and yet profoundly moving. At times I feel as if I am floating above the room, watching from a distance. Every gesture, every word, every intonation speaks of ancient magick.

Jimahl DiFiosa

The Craft is alive, as Morven observed. It has survived for centuries despite every attempt to eradicate it. Now I watch breathlessly as the old oaths are taken once more. As the young priestess takes her solemn pledge, I am reminded again of the enduring power of the Craft.

"I do of my own free will and accord most solemnly swear that I will ever keep secret and never reveal the secrets of the Art," she says. Each word is spoken with unwavering confidence. I can hear the passion for the Craft in her voice.

I remember that three hundred years ago they were hanging witches a few miles from where we now stand. And yet here we are — still here — still invoking the most ancient of Names. Like a tree that pushes through a tiny crack in the pavement of an urban landscape, determined to reach just a piece of sky, our voices are as strong and resilient as ever.

As the new priestess is welcomed into the coven, I remember the words of a poem I had written in the dark half of the year.
"Green growing, future knowing. Seed of summer sown in spring, Conceived by light to rule the darkness, Waken to the words I sing. By rush of wind, by heart's desire, Deep as dark and beyond knowing, Be the fire that makes the magick, Be the green that keeps on growing."

I embrace the newly-made witch fondly and look into her eyes. I see reflected there the joy of a journey begun.

"You are the new generation," I tell her. "You are the future of the Craft. You must carry it on into the new millennium. You must find the secret children of the goddess and freely give them what you have been given. A hundred years from now, someone will be standing where you now are — someone will still be singing the ancient song — the Craft will be as alive and vital as it is right now."

I remember something that Morven told me long ago:
"The goddess will exist only as long as she continues to be invoked.

There must always be a keeper of the mysteries. For when the name of the goddess is forgotten and there is no one left to invoke her — the Craft will cease to exist."

In the impertinent way of a beginner, I did not see the logic in her statement at the time, but now I see clearly that she is right.

And the inherent responsibility that accompanies priesthood is undeniable.

Jimahl DiFiosa

Jimahl DiFiosa

Chapter Thirteen

AFTERTHOUGHTS

A Voice in the Forest

Jimahl DiFiosa

As I complete the task that Alex entrusted to me, there are still many unanswered questions. This, I suppose, is understandable considering that the catalyst for the project has been dead for over a decade.

I never did find Fred, whom Alex remembered fondly at our first communication. Perhaps I will have an opportunity to speak with him at a later date.

The reason for Alex's decision to remain earthbound also eludes me. I can only speculate that he had a vested interest in making certain that the work he began would continue after his death. Although he had apparently named a successor to the role of King of the Witches, that person never stepped forward after Alex's demise. The nature of such a responsibility would inherently include keeping the Alexandrian tradition intact and providing a solid framework for future generations of students. So it is an assumption on my part to wonder if this may have resulted in Alex's last minute decision to stay around for a while and look after his own affairs.

Alex also spoke of a gift that he meant to leave his students at the time of his death. Unfinished business has always seemed the most obvious motive for spirits to remain locked in the space between life and death.

He described this gift in our first encounter as books. Perhaps these are most easily understood as physical volumes, similar to a Book of Shadows. In a small way, the work you are now holding may be a part of Alex's legacy, but perhaps the books that Alex speaks of are not only those which are bound with stitches and glue.

The recurring theme in all of Alex's communications is growth, the preservation of goddess worship, and the critical importance of working together toward a common goal — to secure and maintain the Craft. In this larger sense, I tend to envision the books of which Alex speaks as the cumulative experiences of us all. The pages of such a book become a complex chronicle, a history of many lives — all woven into a magnificent saga. We all contribute to this book whether we realize it or not. Every one of us has a page to write. Each new story is filled with fresh insight and renewed vision. When one page is completed, another is begun. Individually our efforts may seem small and unimportant, but collectively we write a masterpiece — a perpetual story that never ends — because as long as the heart of the Craft beats fiercely, the book of our lives can never truly be finished.

Alex awakened in each of us the slumbering awareness of divine purpose — he reminded us gently that we each have been given a unique gift. In the beginning, our mutual reaction to his attention was much like children around a doting grandparent. "What about me, Alex? Do you have something for me?" And patiently, lovingly, he unfolded each gift in the form of words and gave it over unselfishly.

In retrospect, I realize he also asked each of us for something in return. My own challenge was simply to listen.

Much of Alex's communication seemed to focus on togetherness. When considering the concept of family in any context, it is important to realize that each member of a family is a unique and necessary component of the whole. Without the benefit of our individual experiences and talents, the concept of family quickly solidifies into a rigid, inanimate object — incapable of maintaining a pulse. A spiritual family may be defined as a group of people who share common threads of belief. But a spiritual family is no different than a family in the mundane sense of the word. To say that a spiritual family is defined only by dogma is as ludicrous as saying that a mundane family is composed solely of flesh and bone. Although the commonality of spiritual beliefs serves inarguably as the framework for a healthy group soul, the real test of a family — however defined — is simply how well they care for each other.

Jimahl DiFiosa

I can imagine the Craft as the first bubbling of liquid from an underground stream, the water as sweet and pure as that first tasted by our ancestors. This hidden fountain bubbles up to the surface and forms a pond. It is a deep pond and from the surface it would be easy to dismiss it as stagnant water. But the underground spring feeds the pond well and eventually it trickles over into a small stream. The stream spills lazily through a dry field, giving it new life. On the banks of the stream bloom perennial flowers and, although fragile to the touch, they return year after year in ever greater bursts of color. The stream links to a brook and the brook, diverted in a new direction, slowly becomes a river. And this river flows to another river and the wide expanse of water follows a silent inevitable path to the sea.

I have been as a child in the Craft, standing at that first pond — staring at my reflection in the water and feeling as if I were the only person in the world — disconnected from the whole. But now, as an adult in the Craft, I accept the responsibility of making certain that no one else will be left staring down into that pool of water feeling isolated and alone. I will take them by the hand and show them the ocean — as limitless and as boundless as the love of the goddess.

Like a guardian of a sacred flame, I pass the fire now from my trembling hand to yours. Be vigilant that the fire never goes out.
This, then, is the challenge I leave with each of you. This is the sacred trust.

We must never fail the Craft. We must never fail each other.
As Alex said: "Keep your head up. Keep going."

On the morning of the Summer Solstice I finish the first draft of this manuscript. I give it to Dave who reads through it in one sitting. Dave has persevered through every moment of the project. He has been a consistent source of encouragement to me.

He finishes reading and puts the manuscript down between us. I am pretending not to notice that he's done. I sit opposite him, staring into a cloudy cup of coffee.

"An amazing story," he finally says, "but I think you have to prepare yourself for the fact that some people may find it hard to believe."
"It is an incredible series of events," I admit, "but if I had made the whole thing up I would have definitely written a better ending."
He laughs and pushes the stack of paper across the table.
"There's just one thing missing," he says. "You never did share Alex's last message."

From my weathered notebook, I take out a folded piece of paper and pass it to him. He reads it aloud:

"You sense me near but are unable to touch, to communicate with me, and this frustrates you greatly. I am equally frustrated because I cannot speak to you the way in which you desire. I cannot see you in the way in which you ask me to see you. There are shadows between this world and the next, and — except in a consecrated circle — there is much interference. I hear you. I sense you. But it is difficult for me to speak in return, to touch and to answer your many questions.

"The tie that binds us together is the tie of love for each other. I see the goddess in you and I respond to her. The tie of love that binds us is the love of the Craft that you show forth, and I respond to it as I must.
"I am Alex Sanders. I am he whom you call your forefather. The reason for my presence is clear only to me, for it is a path that I have chosen.

"How long will I remain here? You say there are many who care to listen but in reality there are few who care anymore. There are greater teachers than I to come. I have made a small mark on the face of the cult of the goddess. I would do more if I could.
"My time is up and I must go soon into the void, as you would see it. I pass over soon into the heart of the goddess and from there await rebirth.

"I call you now to service. Be strong in purpose and pure in heart. As long as a circle is cast, as long as the name of the goddess is invoked, she will manifest and grow fat with worship. I cannot say more than that. Never quit. Never stop, for the effort alone carries you forward. Believe in yourself. Believe in the power of your own commitment."

He hands the creased sheet of paper back to me and stands up.

"Let's go for a walk," he says. "It's a beautiful morning."

"Yes." I smile. "It certainly is."

Jimahl DiFiosa

EPILOGUE TO THE FIRST EDITION

A Voice in the Forest

Jimahl DiFiosa

It has been five months since we last spoke with Alex. The time has gone by quickly, much of it spent in preparing this manuscript for publication.

It is exciting to see the Alex Project (as my friends have dubbed it) so close to completion.

Although it was never my intention to write an epilogue, I feel compelled to share a dream I had recently. In this dream, I encounter a mysterious woman who seems to function as a sort of astral receptionist. She delivers a written phone message to me. The slip of paper resembles the usual message forms available in most office environments. It reads simply:

"Please call Alex Sanders at home this evening to discuss the book. You know the number."

When I remember the dream the following morning, I am both amused and surprised. Amused, because once again Alex's gentle sense of humor comes through clearly. Surprised, because I had assumed after the dark April dreams that he is now beyond our reach.

Although it seems unlikely that I will have an opportunity to con- duct additional sessions with the spirit board before this book goes to press, I would encourage the reader to be especially sensitive to Alex's presence and to reach out to him by whatever methods possible.

If there is one thing I've learned through this experience, it is that the living tend to dismiss the dead too readily. Perhaps the boundless chasm that we place between the worlds is one of mortal invention. Perhaps communicating with those who have passed through the veil really is as simple as returning a phone call. So I will end my story by leaving you an open door.

A Voice in the Forest

If, while you read this final page, you sense someone standing just behind you, don't be hasty to give your 'overactive imagination' all the credit.

In the realm of witchcraft, anything is possible.

Jimahl, October 1999

Jimahl DiFiosa

Jimahl DiFiosa

THE LAMMAS SESSION 2002

A Voice in the Forest

Jimahl DiFiosa

It is late in July and we have returned to the Lammas woods. There are fewer of us now. We are getting older and for some of us camping is no longer the novelty that it once was. I suppose there comes a time in everyone's life when all the toasted marshmallows in the world can't make sleeping on the ground an adventure again. The campers who remain among us would like to think we are pioneers at heart, but even we have made small concessions to comfort, such as inflatable air mattresses between our backs and the cold earth.

This summer evening, as we hurry to pitch our tents before dark, I am with Morven, Aria, Fuschia and Thorn. Morven, of course, is the constant. She has always been there for me, a friend for the record books. Aria is my friend and student. She is a powerhouse of occult energy. I have just raised her to third degree at Mid-Summer. The pages of our ritual were taken from some recently discovered journals written by Alex Sanders. In it we enacted the rise and fall of the lost continent of Atlantis. I was the old priest, anxious to pass on the power and knowledge of a doomed civilization to a young and eager apprentice. She became the High Priestess, to whom the keys of the kingdom were passed. How appropriate the ritual was to my current state of mind. Turning fifty this year, and maybe being just a bit crankier than usual, I am focused more than ever on finding my true spiritual purpose.

For me the past year has been an adventure into a world where anything can happen. I have spent months following a personal trail of bread crumbs into the past. One particular journey, prompted by my work with Alex, ended deep in a Mexican jungle when, with a shaman's help, I came face to face with the 600-year-old grave of a Mayan priest. My grave, so the shaman said. And suddenly I understood how two life-times – one past and one present – can come together again like two ends of a single cord. I wrote in my journal at the time:

"I finally understand the big picture. If this is all there is, it is more than enough. And if there is more to come in my life, I can only imagine what wonders lie ahead."

Fuschia and Thorn are a couple and seem as comfortable together as if they shared the same body. She is Morven's witch-sister — both of them were initiated into the same coven many years ago. Fuschia bears an uncanny resemblance to a 70s rock star, so much so that she gets stopped on the street and asked for autographs. Her husband is a lean, handsome man hopelessly in love with both her and the Craft. He will take his initiation at the coming Equinox.

I finish staking down my tent and pause to look around the familiar landscape. Do the woods look smaller or is it my imagination? Or maybe it's like the perpetually shifting memories of a child growing up too fast – nothing quite looks the same as it did from the back seat of your parent's car. Is the world getting smaller or am I getting taller? I used to rhyme as I shot up out of my sneakers into the complex world of adulthood – a world in which everyone expected you to know where you were going, but in which no one had a map.

Someone once asked me what happens as I go into trance. It is hard to explain — the changes that occur seem to be more external than internal. There is usually a feeling that I am becoming larger than my environment. In the forest, these shifts in perception are more acute. I can describe it only as a softening of the physical world around me. For example, I look at a tree and it is no longer a solid object. The edges of it blur like a watercolor painting over which someone has passed a wet brush. This is usually followed by a slow fade to black, like a movie screen when the film is over. And in the dark is his voice, his face. Alex. He stands there smiling. His smile is often sad. Or maybe it's just me filtering him. Maybe I'm the sad one. I don't know....

By 2002 we are all aware that he is once again physically reincarnate and has been for over two years. I shared a few clues in the first edition of Voice — clues provided by Alex himself while he was between the worlds.

He told us that he would reincarnate in the year 2000, that his mother would not be British, and that she would be a witch.

There was more of course — so much more that none of us would dare put into print and probably never will. Among other bits of information, Alex told us that he would reincarnate as a male, and he told us the date the child would be born and the name his mother would give to him. This information was provided during a spirit board session in October 1998.

We all understood the enormity of the picture Alex had drawn. The burden of that knowledge splintered the group in many ways. Many of us, I'm sure, had hoped it was all a strange coincidence, but even those of us who understood it to be true realized that there was no possible way any of us could ever act on the information he had provided.

How difficult it is even now to understand how any of this is possible. Life and death are not in and of themselves a tough concept. An ending and a beginning — easy to grasp with linear thought — but when two lifetimes collide, when the spirit of a man reincarnates into a boy, and the memory of the man's life is still intact — when he can still communicate with friends of his former self while his spirit inhabits the body of the child — this presents a much more complicated picture of the afterlife. And suddenly all of what you think you know gets lost in translation. All the rules change. Walls and doors, windows and floors — it all fades away. There are no boundaries anymore. Nothing can ever be the same.

It is dark now in our Lammas woods and Thorn builds a fire. We cook a simple meal and share it in silence. The woods are quiet. Soon the sense that Alex is drawing near is overwhelming. It is as if he knows exactly where we'll be the last weekend of July, as if there is a homing device attached to us — a beacon that flips into full alert and projects a bridge of light between the astral and the physical. Or perhaps it is the place itself. The woods seem haunted now, 'fairy haunted,' as Aria says.

Morven brings the spirit board to the picnic table. Fuschia sits across from me and places her hands on the planchette. Her fingers touch mine. I've worked with her as a medium once before when her mother died suddenly and Fuschia needed to understand why the departed spirit was restless. Thorn sits nearby. He seems anxious to hear from Alex. Morven sits next to me with a pad of paper, ready as always to act as scribe. Aria, a perennial camper, sits comfortably in a camp chair next to the fire. She is wrapped in a deep green cloak.

"Is there anybody there?" I ask.

CL O S E

"Who are you?"

F RI EN D

"Are you known to someone here?"

N EX T

"Are you a spirit of someone recently deceased?"

ET

"...phone home," Fuschia jokes and we all laugh. I sense that this spirit is not going to be a significant contact.

"Are you tied to somebody that is here?"

There is no answer. We dismiss 'ET' and start again. This time, instead of calling out to Alex verbally, I reach out to him psychically. He responds to my silent call immediately.

Jimahl DiFiosa

BLESSINGS

"Alex, I want to introduce you to Thorn. He's new to the Craft."

T H O RN O T HERS

Alex always acts the perfect gentleman in these sessions, politely acknowledging everyone present as if he physically walked into the room.

"Is there anyone you want to send a message to?"

W O MA N

"What woman?"

RX

... and then in his familiar way of emphasizing a response, YES Alex only uses YES to emphasize an important message, so I feel this must be significant. Morven and I recognize the initials of a mutual friend. Her name is Raokhsha, a Gardnerian high priestess, and the person who originally invited us to join her on a Lammas weekend in 1998. I would finally understand the 'connection' in the fall of 2003. In the final stages of preparing this second edition for publication I would receive an unexpected note from Raokhsha:

"Although I have been far out on the periphery of your experience with Alex — being three campsites away when you first sat down with the spirit board — two things just blinked on in my brain. I remember first inviting you to 'the forest,' and your reluctance to come to what you thought would be a hedonistic pagan fiasco. But you came, you found the 'bravery within,' and you chanced a couple of nights in a strange contraption called a tent on the cold lumpy ground in a summer-lasts-only-until-July-17th section

A Voice in the Forest

of the world. There was the 'acclimation pathworking' that took us all into the 'magickal forest,' and you decided that it wasn't going to be a half-bad adventure.

"When you wrote yesterday that you thought that there was no longer a reason to return to the woods, it seemed more than coincidental that I, too, had decided that my own time in 'Lammas ville' was over and that I probably wouldn't be coming back to New Hampshire. I have been ambivalent about making the trip again, feeling that 'my work here is done.' Then a gong went off and I thought: All these years I hadn't recognized that maybe part of my 'mission' to create the Lammas gatherings was to lure one 'Jimahl di Fiosa' into the woods to fulfill a mission of his own."

"What message should we give her?" I ask.

B EL I EVEI N S EL F

Before I can ask anything else, Alex adds quickly:

A REY O UT EA C HI N G

"Are you talking to someone in particular, Alex? " ALL

"Yes, we are all teaching." It wasn't entirely true from my perspective, but I knew it is the answer he wanted to hear. This is a hot issue with Alex.

A G EI S N O T

He doesn't complete this sentence, although I sense he means to say that age is not a factor – that we all must continue to teach.

"Alex, have you reincarnated?"

YES

Jimahl DiFiosa

"How is it still possible for you to communicate?"

WHEN RES T I N G

"When the child is resting?"

YES

"Are you happy with all the work we have done since the first communication with you four years ago?"

OK

I am a little taken aback by his lackluster response. Just OK? "Alex, what else can we do? Do you have anything to tell us?"

C HA N N EL

I suddenly get a fresh jolt of energy. It is about as subtle as taking a sip of water from a fire hose. Fuschia, however, seems to be getting tired. She worries aloud that she will lose the connection and asks "Alex, do you want us to change the channel?" She meant, of course, that someone else should take her spot.

S T UDEN T S

Alex is always talking about students and the need to keep teaching others about the Craft. I decide to change the subject and ask him if he has personal messages for anyone present.

"Do you have a message for Morven?"

D A RL I N G

Alex frequently uses terms of endearment when referring to his priestesses.

"Do you have a message for Aria?"

A R I A I S B E A U T I F U L N A M E

"Do you have a message for me, Alex?" Fuschia asks.

F US C HI A

"We love you so much," she responds. "We miss you."

HEL L O RI N G

"What should we ring?" Fuschia asks.

B E A L (bell?)

"Alex, can you see us?" I ask. "Are you here on this plane right now?"
F I RE

Thorn nods in the direction of the campfire. We can hear shuffling on the other side of the fire. It is as if Alex is physically standing in the shadows, pacing back and forth.

"Alex, we welcome you. Do you have a message for Morganna?" (This is a reference to a dear friend, a magnificent Alexandrian high priestess, Morganna Davies, coauthor of the book Keepers of the Flame.)

WI T C HC RA F T I S HERL I F E

"Alex, Morganna is traveling to England soon. Is there anything important for her to do while in England?" This question comes from Fuschia.

N EA T HT O RL O O KF O RA S I G N

Jimahl DiFiosa

"Do you have a message for me, Alex?" I ask, already knowing the answer.

T E A C H

"Teach? Alex, can I have a new message? I've stopped teaching for now. Is it okay if Aria is my last student?"

NO

Alex tries unsuccessfully to push through a long message. It keeps getting jumbled up on the board and yet seems terribly important. I sense that he is trying to speak to Morven about something she must do for him. The more jumbled the letters become, the more frustrated he gets.

C O T H E M WAT E A M E A

"I don't understand," Morven responds. "Alex, say it simply."

C O I N MEMO RI A L

Fuschia and Morven receive a psychic impression that the word is meant to be translated from the French 'coin' to the English 'corner.' They try to make sense of the message in this context, but can't quite understand. I decide to focus on the word 'memorial' instead. "You want Morven to do a memorial?" I ask.

A C I V E (archive?)

"Who is the memorial for?"

ME

"What do you want me to do?" Morven asks.

L EA VEA P L A C EF O RMEI N Y O UR C I R C L ES

A Voice in the Forest

"Like Morganna's coven?" Morven asks. (Morganna always sets up a small altar in her circles, with a photo of Alex and a rose.)

HEA L Y O URS EL VES I N T HEC RA F T B ET O G ET HE RI N L O VES T A YS T R O N G N EVERMA KEMA G I C K WI T HO

UT MEI N Y O UR C I R C L ES

This flurry of very articulate direction leaves the atmosphere extremely charged. The last bit of communication was delivered in an aggressive way. There is no room for doubt here. These are not suggestions — they are demands. Fuschia decides to lighten the mood by asking Alex a technical question. Earlier in the day she was musing aloud why it was that everyone seemed to gravitate toward copper pentacles instead of some other metal.

"Alex," she asked, "why is the pentacle copper? Is it because it's conductive?"

A L L A WI T C HHA D

"That was the only thing available? Could other metals be used?"

A L L S A MEP URP O S E

My psychic sense is that Alex is stymied for a minute.

He was on a roll and then sidetracked by framing responses to Fuchia's technical question. There is an awkward period of silence as if he is thinking, "Where was I?" Thorn decides to speak up for the first time at this point.

"Is my initiation the right path for me?" he asks.

YES L O VEB EG I N I N G S

I am receiving a lot of psychic information from Alex at this point. It's as if he wants to speak, but the board is too slow a vehicle. I'm sure he would write through me if I had paper and pen, but it is too dark. So what I get instead are images, thoughts, impressions, but all at once — they are hard for me to sort through, to separate, to explain.

I start to shake and tears well in my eyes. I try to explain to the others that he is sad and very frustrated. He feels that no one is working together anymore. Then I see, from his vantage point, coven after coven of witches — all set apart from each other — no one is talking to each other — and yet each one of them has a piece of Alex — maybe it's a memory, a bit of paper, something, and all the puzzle pieces of knowledge, if put together, would have an incredible impact. But no one sees the possibility. If everyone just came together with one purpose we could work miracles, but instead we are like children who stab at the dark with forks and knives to keep our fears at bay. We try to make a big picture out of a million small ones.

"He wants to be a part of this," I say. "He wants everyone to realize that he is still here — still able to do what maybe he failed to do in his lifetime — to bring us all together — one heart, one soul..." One giant step for mankind... Oh crap, it all seems so impossible — it will never work, Alex — we're all too territorial — one tradition doesn't speak to the other and there are those without any teaching at all — orphans of the Craft — what is to become of the young ones who can't be taught? I can't understand all of what I'm feeling. I can only sense that he wants all of us who worship the Goddess to come to some common terms. He sees a Utopian world in which this is not only possible, but necessary for the survival of the Craft. There is also an ego involved. He's really upset because there are those who use his name as a qualifier, but who do not remember him.

I don't know how much of this is said, how much of it is thought. But I end up sobbing, holding onto the planchette, but feeling as if I am falling through a void.

A Voice in the Forest

"Alex," Morven asks, "is what Jimahl says true?"

ALLBELIEVEINGODDESS

"You say we're all the same?" she asks.

YES

"Why?" she persists.

G O DDES S

This word practically jumps off the board. I hear it in my head. It is both an invocation and a scream. What is so difficult to understand? he seems to be saying. We are all children of the Goddess. How is one person or one group of people better or worse than any other?

"Alex," Morven continues in a quiet soothing voice, "is it important to maintain oaths?"

MA KERES T UN DERS T A N D

"But what about our oaths?" she presses.

DEA DI N W A T ER

I am fading now. The shadows around me are closing in. I don't think I can do this much longer.

Fuschia stares back at me from just a few feet away, and yet it is like she is looking at me from another time.

"What's dead?" Morven asks.

GODDESSALLPEOPLE

"But isn't it important that the Alexandrian tradition stays intact?" she continues.

BESTRONGNEVERSTOP

"Alex, I still don't understand," Morven says. I can see how badly she wants to understand and I can sense him lean into her, as if he is embracing his high priestess.

HOLYTASKFORMEGONENEVERDIE

"Alex, could you be more specific?" she asks again.

BEALIGHTABEACONRARESOMEONECARESSOMUCH

Aria has gotten up from her seat by the fire and is standing next to Morven.

"Alex, I can help. What would you have me do?" she asks.

OPENHEARTTOTRUTHOPENSELFTOPOWER

I sense that he is withdrawing now. He spells out:

GONOWREST

"Alex," I ask, "are you still going to be available to us?"

HAVEFAITH

At this point, I sense that the energy is gone and I release the planchette.

Surprisingly, in the months that follow, the four of us spoke very little about this experience. I spun my wheels for a while trying to figure out what he meant by the reference to the 'coin memorial.' One day I found a reference in Greek mythology to Charon, the ferryman of the dead. Souls are brought to him by Hermes and he ferries them across the river in exchange for a coin. For this reason, a coin was traditionally placed under the tongue or over the eyes of the deceased before burial. According to the myth, if someone didn't have the coin to pay the ferryman, their soul was doomed to wander the earth for a hundred years. In a strange kind of way, I thought, perhaps Alex needed such a passage before he could finally be at rest. I started to devise an elaborate ritual in which I would offer a coin on his behalf to the ferryman. Paul and Phoenix listened patiently to my ranting and then gently talked me away from the ledge.

"Jimahl," Paul reasoned, "Alex is such an adept. Think about it — he doesn't need your help to cross the Abyss. Besides, he's already reincarnate."

"But the coin reference makes sense to me. This seems pretty simple. I just go into a deep trance and get out onto the astral. Then I find the river and explain it all to the ferryman."

"No offense, Jimahl, but that is most definitely not a good idea," Phoenix interjected. "You're way off on this one. Did you ever think that by helping him across the river you will silence him forever. He obviously has his own reasons for the path he has chosen. Why can't you just let well enough alone?"

"But what if I'm right? What if he needs someone to pay his passage. Look, if I'm wrong, the ferryman will understand. I'll just come back."

"Jimahl," Phoenix said in an exasperated tone, "let me explain this to you in a way that is easy for you to understand. If you do this ritual — you will die."

"Oh." I acquiesce.

Jimahl DiFiosa

He has a good point. I can walk away from this idea.

Jimahl DiFiosa

♂
THE LAMMAS SESSION 2003

DEAD IN THE WATER

A Voice in the Forest

Jimahl DiFiosa

This phrase, used by Alex last summer, has been haunting me for weeks.

At first I thought it was meant to describe something dead which floats in the water — a bird, a fish, a person. But as nautical jargon it means something quite different. It refers to a vessel that is making no progress. The sea is still. There are no waves. The air is still. There is no wind.

Is that how he sees the Craft today? I wonder if have we lost momentum, direction — not even drifting aimlessly because, even then, we would ultimately arrive somewhere.

When I think of Alex now, there is an immediate connection. There is no need to pull out the tarot or spirit board. He is somehow nearer than he has ever been and at the same time farther away.

When Morven calls to ask if I am willing to return once more to the Lammas woods, she already knows my answer. We decide to make a weekend of it and invite some of the others to join us. It is a good excuse for a reunion of old friends, we reason. Many decline the invitation — the drive is too far, the weather too unpredictable, their lives too busy — and yet I know that the real reason for at least some of them is that they no longer see a point in continuing this communication. There is an ethical stew brewing. If we know that there is a young child involved, and if there is the slightest possibility that trying to communicate with Alex will harm the child, then why continue? I agree on principle and yet remain convinced that Alex can speak, or not speak, for himself. And so it is one year later when I return to New Hampshire with Morven. I meet her at a suburban bus stop late on a July afternoon and pile my gear into the back seat of her car. The drive into the country is restful. It is a beautiful summer day. Wildflowers are in bloom along the highway.
Fuschia and Thorn agree to meet us there later that evening. They will be delayed in their journey by an accident — a landscaping truck overturned

on the narrow mountain road, spilling boulders across the highway. When they do finally arrive, Morven and I have already eaten dinner and are sharing a bottle of wine. This is our private ritual each Lammas — two friends, two glasses, and a bottle of expensive cabernet. With the late arrival of Fuschia and Thorn, as well as two other witches who accepted our invitation at the last minute, there is a lot of activity in the campsite. The newcomers are Iymlad and Uinen — two of Morganna's students. They seem to be the outdoor type, completely at home in the forest. I am happy that they've decided to join us. Their enthusiasm for the Craft is refreshing.

This may be the last time I visit these woods. There is a different feeling in the air. To use Alex's analogy, perhaps the dead water is beginning to stir again. It is easy to get all poetic when you're sitting beneath a grove of old trees at night. The moon has just gone new — like it was on that very first Lammas when Alex came to us. Iymlad and Uinen build an altar for Alex on the stump of a fallen tree. They place a photograph of him there — it is from an old book, a picture of a young and handsome man who stands barefoot and robed inside a ceremonial circle, his sword raised in invocation. They place a red candle and a plastic cup of beer before the photograph.

"I know you guys like to give him wine," Iymlad says, smiling, "but I really think he prefers beer."

As the sun sinks behind the trees and the shadows of the overhead branches get long and cool, Alex's face is illuminated by the candle. Red seems appropriate to me, as I watch the hot wax pool on the stump and drip onto the ground. Red is the color of love, so says the table of correspondences — not infatuation, but eternal love — love that passes all tests and overcomes all obstacles.

I know how badly Iymlad and Uinen both want to speak with Alex, but his spirit doesn't come on that first night or even the second night. I try to pull him in, but there is nothing. The following morning they have to return home. I hug them both as they leave the campground.

"Maybe next year," Iymlad says. I wonder if there will be a next year.

Then, on our last evening in the woods, there seems to be a change in the astral climate. I am sitting comfortably, reading a book, when Alex seems to settle in beside me. "I think we can do this now," I say to Morven and she gets up quickly to retrieve the spirit board from her tent. Fuschia and Thorn join us at the old wooden table. Morven will remember afterward that it was exactly one year ago to the day when we last spoke to Alex. By the time Fuschia's hands join mine on the planchette, I am already feeling the connection. This gentle shift from one reality to another has become as comfortable now as putting on a pair of old slippers. The sensation is almost fluid, as if warm tea were running through my veins. Fuschia is smiling. We all expect something good to happen. Morven acts again as scribe and Thorn begins to build a campfire. He knows that Alex likes the fire.

"Let's go, Alex," I say aloud. "I know we can do this one more time." As before, I ask most of the questions. "If Alex Sanders is present, we ask you to acknowledge us. Alex, are you there?"

N EA R

"Are you the spirit of Alex Sanders?"

ABO Y

Oh no, is this the boy? Is he dead? But then I realize that it is the spirit of a child much older — not connected to Alex in any way. This frequently happens when a spirit board is used — much like turning on a radio and then going through the act of tuning into a clear signal.

"What is your name?"

PETE

"Do you have anything you want to say to us?"

NEAR

"Pete, how old are you?"

9

"Do you know you're dead?"

"Please what?"

PLEASE

FIND MAMA

Fuschia lets out a small cry. "You're looking for your mother?"

YES

"Do you know when you died?" I ask.

I can see that Fuschia is disturbed by this unexpected contact with a dead child who is searching for his mother. Not to sound insensitive, but I have made a conscious effort in the past year to develop my skills as a medium and working with confused spirits comes with the job.

1 92 8

"Pete, you're dead, and your mother's dead, too. Do you realize that?"

YES

Not so long ago I would have spent half the night helping this boy find his mother, but now I know that love is what binds us together after death. If he loves his mother and she loves him, then nothing will keep them apart. Sometimes all it takes is for someone to remind the dead that love never dies.

"We're going to release you now," I say to the child. "Go to your mother.

She is waiting for you. You can see her — just open your eyes and look."

We wait a few minutes and then try again.
"We want to speak to Alex Sanders, and only Alex Sanders."

AT REST

There is an unexpected edge to his energy. I sense that he is preoccupied.

"Are we bothering you?" I ask.

FUSCHIA

"Hi, Alex," she responds, looking at me nervously.
Something's different. What is it? I try to improve the connection. "Alex, I know this is you. I know your energy."

H E L L O M O R V E N

"Hello, Alex," Morven responds.

G O D D E S S L O V E T O M E (...and after a long pause) L O V E

"Alex," I note, "your energy is different. Are you still incarnate in the boy?"

Y O U K N O W T O G E T H E R

"Alex, the child should be three years old. Is that right?"

A Voice in the Forest

N EWS I N HO UR

I get the impression that he is brushing us off — telling us to come back in an hour. It doesn't make any sense to me. His energy starts to pull back. "Alex, I think we're losing you. Can you answer a few questions?"

A B IT

"Alex, do you know that I'm doing an expanded edition of your book?"

ST A R T "Yes, I've started planning."

B EL I EVE

"Do you have anything new to tell us tonight?"

Y O UEV

"Alex, what is it?"

V

"Do you have any messages to share?"

This question seems to renew the contact for a few minutes. Alex mentions many people by name — some of whom we don't know. He asks after his family — his former wife Maxine, their children whom he calls by name, and his old friend Loriel.

"Alex, Loriel is writing a piece for the new book."

DO IT S O O N

"Do you have a message for him?"

Jimahl DiFiosa

ASK HIM TO TELL YOU ABOUT FIRST

"I know, Alex. He told me." (Loriel's initiation was witnessed by Stewart Farrar and was featured in an article in "Reveille." I know that Alex must be proud of this, as he provided Farrar with his first exposure to witchcraft. Who could have foreseen that he would eventually seek initiation himself and that he would become such a prolific author of books on the Craft — books that no doubt have played a significant role in the resurgence of Wicca around the world.)

Alex moves on to mention the name of a woman whom none of us know. It's as if he is flipping through an old address book of acquaintances, saying whatever comes to mind.
"What message do you have for her, Alex?' I ask, expecting something profound.

MARRIED A FOOL

We are surprised by this remark. I think one comes to expect that the deceased are more forgiving than the living — but in a strange way it is endearing to realize that Alex still says exactly what's on his mind without regard to protocol. "Alex," I joke, "that's mean-spirited. Why do you say that?"

BIGOT

"Bigoted against whom?"

ALEX

He moves on quickly to mention the names of other friends. To each of these he sends warm regards. They are obviously people whom he still cares about a great deal. But one thing troubles me — and it is very subtle — I'm not sure any of the others have noticed. In his response to my last

A Voice in the Forest

question, he refers to himself in the third person. This is the first time in all of our communication that he's done this.

"Do you have messages for anyone else?"

GYPSY

We are all familiar with Gypsy. She is an Alexandrian high priestess and a talented singer. She and her husband own a popular mail order business, as well as an occult shop in eastern Massachusetts.
"What message do you have for Gypsy?"

P L EA S E HEL P HI M

"Who, Alex?"

Alex proceeds to spell out the name of an old friend of his from England — a man that Morven had met years before.
"Alex, do you mean your friend from the UK, who came to visit me?"

YES

"Help him with what?" Morven asks.

VES HO S HO

"Alex, you're not making sense," I say.

F RI EN D

"What does Gypsy have to do?"

GY P S Y H E L P

"Is this man still living?"

YES

"Is he in some sort of trouble?"

F RI EN D

"Alex, we know he's your friend, but what is Gypsy supposed to do?" I am already thinking ahead to what promises to be a very strange phone call to Gypsy. There are a few more details that Alex provides about his troubled friend, and then the energy starts to wane.
"Alex, we're losing you."

W A I T A HO UR

"For what?"

L A D YS R I A H

"Alex, you're not making sense. Wait an hour for what?"

N IT E

At this point, we stop and discuss what Alex could mean. I think that the lost connection is circumstantial — some congestion on the astral perhaps — and suggest we wait a few minutes and try again. Fuschia disagrees. She says an hour means an hour. Alex seems adamant that we should wait and she doesn't want to upset him.

The mechanics of communicating with Alex have admittedly become more complex now that the boy is getting older. It is obvious to us that Alex can only communicate effectively when the boy is asleep. I look at my watch. According to the geographic references Alex has provided in previous sessions, he is currently inhabiting a time zone several hours away from us. I comment that perhaps the boy was stirred from slumber by a dream.

"Maybe he's dreaming of us," Thorn says quietly. We laugh, but Thorn's comment gets me thinking about the inevitable confusion that the child will face as he continues to mature. How can Alex continue to occupy even a small part of his sleeping consciousness?

We wait a few minutes and then I insist on trying again. Fuschia states for the record that she feels we should wait a full hour before trying again, but I allow my ego to take the upper hand. I am angry that Alex put us off and intend to tell him so.

"He needs to lose the attitude," I say to Fuschia. "I don't see anyone else still trying to communicate with him."

"Jimahl," she warns as I place the planchette between us, "don't piss him off. He's not kidding around."

We try again but nothing happens. We encounter 'radio silence,' as I jokingly call a dead astral connection.

"I told you so," Fuschia says.

We wait about forty minutes and then I want to try again.

"Jimahl, I don't have a good feeling about this," Fuschia states. "It hasn't been an hour yet. We have to wait twenty more minutes."

"This is ridiculous. I don't understand what his problem is tonight."

We place the planchette on the spirit board and try once more to renew the contact.

"We want to speak to Alex Sanders. Alex, it's us again."

B E P A T I EN T

At this point, we all realize that Alex is serious, that we need to wait, so we talk amongst ourselves and give it another twenty minutes.

It is now exactly an hour later. Fuschia gets a psychic impression that we should set out cheese and wine, which we do. To me it seems like a peace offering, given Alex's earlier mood.

"Alex, are you available now?" I ask cautiously.

AT R E S T

"Do you mean this is a good time?"

BED

"The boy is napping?"

YES

"We have food and wine for you."

WEL C O ME

In an instant, all the tension of our previous attempts melts away. It is as if we all take a deep breath in unison — as if the child is asleep, the house is quiet. Alex's energy is once again warm and gracious. I joke that it can't be easy for him to be an adult stuck in the body of a three-year-old. It must make those late night cravings for a pint of ale really difficult.

"Thank you for coming back to us, Alex. Can we ask you a few more questions?"

A GA I N

"Do you have a message for the children of the goddess?"

WAT C H D E V O T E L I F E TO

Maybe it was the late hour, but Alex was having difficulty finishing a sentence.

A Voice in the Forest

"Is there anything you want to tell us?" ARWAEM

"You're not making any sense, Alex." I suddenly sense that he wants to give us each personal messages. Do you have a message for Thorn?"

A G O O DMA N

HEL I KES T O MA S T ER C RA F T

This is a message with a dual meaning, so characteristic of Alex's wit. Thorn is not only now an initiate of the Craft, he is also a craftsman by trade.

"Any message for Morven?"

B EMYHEA R T S DES I RE

"For Fuschia?"

B EL I EVEI N Y O URS EL F

"Alex, do you have a message for Morganna? Are you happy with the work she has done for you?" (As Alex had predicted, Morganna did receive a sign while visiting Glastonbury Tor last autumn — three small shafts of wheat. What they mean is still a mystery to all of us.)

MY B E L I E V E R U A RE L I G H T

"Any message for me?" I ask, all the while thinking: Please Alex, anything but 'teach'....

ST A Y O F F L E F T P A TH

His message shocks the others and embarrasses me, although I understand immediately what he means. In the past year I have all but retired from Wicca and have been experimenting with more arcane magick. While not an overtly left-hand path, it is admittedly left of center field from a typical white light perspective. There is always an intrinsic danger to swimming in deep water, I reason. I make a mental note to heed Alex's advice.

"Are you here with us tonight?"

KI N DO F

The connection is strained again. It is taking a lot of energy to keep it live.

"Is there anything we can do to forge a stronger link with this boy?"

O L DS O UL

"Alex, I'm sensing that we're on the verge of losing the ability to speak with you. Is there anything we can do?"

NO

"Alex, is there anything else you want to say to us while we can still communicate?"

RA RET HA T Y O UC A RES O MUC H BEWELL

S T A YT R UET O C RA F T

The connection ends abruptly.

The following morning we get up, take down our tents, and hug each other good-bye. With autumn just ahead and a long cold winter to follow, we make no pretenses about how soon we're likely to see each other again. I spend the next few months working on the expanded edition of VOICE. It is important to me that I include the details of these last few sessions.

A Voice in the Forest

I have many questions that go unanswered until Willow comes to me with her research into the subject of tulkus, spirits of incarnate teachers. In Buddhist spirituality, these deceased teachers not only have the adeptness to choose where and when they will reincarnate, but often use divination to assist their students in identifying them in their new life.

So there's a name for this phenomenon. That should make me happy. But ironically it only saddens me more. There is no provision in Wicca for this type of situation. So what is the point of even knowing about it? No one I know is going to knock on some stranger's door with an armload of gifts for the baby. What a strange situation Alex has gotten himself into.

It is now late in October and the tide of All Hallows is rising again. One night, as the full moon rides high above the city, I find it unusually hard to sleep. There are shadows in my dreams and an unsettled feeling when I awake. I finally get tired of tossing from one side of the bed to the other and get up just before dawn. I suddenly have 'all these words' rising to the hazy surface of consciousness, so I find a pad of paper and sit scribbling in the half-light.

"We see goddess, but is that all there is? We see god, but is that all there is? Why do we constantly seek to give a name to what can't be named, a face to what has no face. The only face that matters is the one staring back at us through time gone, time remembered. There is nothing — absolutely nothing — more devastating than loss of purpose — when we cease to believe in the power of our dreams, we cease to exist. All that remains is the now, and within the context of now, there can be no future. We must continue to push ahead, to believe in ourselves, to see the future, to have a vision of what comes next. We must perpetually ask the question: what comes next?

"We must continue to probe the dark for the answer. If we fail to do this, we assimilate the mistakes of the past into the present and our condition becomes hopeless. For what is stagnant is spoiled. What is inert has no life. What has no life is dead. The secret is that there is never a need to be dead. The soul lives forever. The soul alone dictates what comes next.

A life lived purposefully is a life worth living. No one should die without purpose. To do so condemns one to an eternity of regret." I sit staring at the pad of paper for a while. I want to think it's Alex again — that it's still possible for him to filter through the complicated state of affairs that he has created. But part of me believes that it is over. That what comes next is our move. There are no more signs, no more mysteries — just a lot of hard work for those who still care enough to want to make a difference. Or maybe the truth is that all the caring in the world can't make that much of a difference. I guess we each have to decide for ourselves whether any of this is worth the effort. Perhaps we are like children ourselves — children who try to see the universe in the head of a dandelion. Blow too hard and it all falls apart.

In the final resolve, I know I have to walk away from further communication through the child. I wish the boy and his mother well. I hope he grows up to enjoy life and to live in a world that is uniquely his own. And still I wonder — will some part of Alex remain hidden deep inside his soul? Will he look one day at a map of the United States and put his finger on a small New England town and wonder why he has a sudden urge to go there? Will his first imaginary friend be named 'Alex'? Perhaps it would help if I leave a fresh trail of bread crumbs for him to follow. Maybe he or his mother, or someone who loves them, will find this book.

You were born on May Eve in the year 2000. Your mother named you after a magician — a character in children's books.

No, it's too much to hope for — the best that can happen is that you have a long and healthy life, that you stay safe in your own world — a world where there is no 'Jimahl' or 'Morven,' or sacred groves in the woods where old friends gather.

A world without pubs and British accents and strange people doing even stranger things.

A Voice in the Forest

A world where there is only 'Harry.'

And that should be more than enough for one lifetime.

Blesséd be.

Jimahl DiFiosa

Jimahl DiFiosa

☿
EPILOGUE FOR THE SECOND EDITION

A Voice in the Forest

Jimahl DiFiosa

When people ask me what's new since I finished writing A Voice in the Forest, I avoid the question as much as possible. Not because nothing is new, but because nothing is the same. The completion of the book coincided with, or was more than likely the catalyst for, changes on so many levels of my life that it is difficult to frame a coherent response to the question without sounding like a babbling idiot.

A few months after the first edition of Voice went to print, I visited a psychic at the suggestion of my friend Aria. Coming from someone who is just coming into their own as a medium, it may sound surprising that I try to avoid psychics. I tend to be quite skeptical of the information they provide, which can usually be summed up under the category "Things the Customer Wants to Hear." In fact, I have only known two true psychics in my lifetime — and one of them is this woman, whom I'll call Teresa.

I sat with her one rainy afternoon in the parlor of her house. She took one look at me and asked a simple question. "Are you happy?" I was surprised by the question and reacted defensively. "Of course I'm happy," I fired back and immediately started a mental checklist of the proofs — good health, great job, long term relationship, just published my first book.... She took my hand and looked at my palm, tracing the lines there with her long fingernails. "You're not happy," she said. "You think you are, but you are actually very unhappy. I see you in a temple, a sacred place. You will journey very far to find this temple and yet arrive there quite unexpectedly. After this journey, it all changes. You will lose everything that you have come to believe is stable. You will suffer more than you've ever imagined. But after the pain come new revelations. You are a very old soul. You will meet other old souls and with their help you will find your true spiritual purpose." I remember staring at her in disbelief. What the hell was that all about? She didn't even mention my book!
In the months that followed, the events of my life unraveled exactly as she predicted. My partner of 18 years started working for a travel company.

One day he came home with complimentary tickets for a Mexican vacation. The exclusive resort was situated on the coast of the Yucatan peninsula. There was little to do except lie around a pool and work on the tan. By the sixth day into the trip, we were feeling a little bored. A local sightseeing company was offering a tour of the ruins of Chichen Itza, a nearby Mayan ceremonial center. I agreed to go along only from a Discovery Channel point of view, as I had not yet equated my current state of affairs in any way with Teresa's strange predictions. Consequently, I was unprepared for the sudden impact that this excursion would have on me, and the redirection of my spiritual life that would follow.

In the center of the ancient city, there is a temple to the Mayan god Kulkulkan, the legendary feathered serpent. It is a tall pyramid, with narrow steps. There is a rope tied to the middle of these steps to assist terrified tourists in navigating the steep incline. Immediately upon seeing that the temple was open for climbing, I remember running effortlessly to the top of the pyramid. The view from the top was incredible. Looking out over the ancient city, I felt as if I had come home again. My descent from the pyramid was equally effortless. While others clung tenaciously to the rope, I walked down the stone steps completely upright, my eyes straight ahead. It was as if my feet knew instinctively where to go.

It seemed as if I had done this before. A pervasive sense of *déja vu* overwhelmed me. An eagle soared above my head, screeching loudly. And then suddenly from a cloudless late afternoon sky, came dark glowering thunderheads. Flashes of lightning forked down into the treetops. I managed to get off the pyramid before the deluge — driving torrents of rain that quickly flooded the flat plain on which the ancient city sits. The storm lasted over two hours. I had never seen such rain — the ruts in the dirt road and the low-lying parts of the grassy fields quickly turned into swirling puddles. I heard — actually sensed with my whole body — the jungle around me, breathing.

When the rain finally stopped, I walked out into the field that stretched out beneath the great pyramid. The air was filled with the sound of singing frogs. Their voices were deafening, it was if the storm had just woken a whole frog kingdom from sleep. Then I heard the sound of a conch being blown. It was an unmistakable sound. I saw a Mayan priest standing at the very edge of the uppermost temple. He was dressed in a beautiful feathered robe. I assumed it was some kind of historic pageant that was enacted for the tourists. But when I commented on the figure to my partner, he reacted only with an uncomfortable stare. The priest was obviously something that only I could see.

Months later I would connect the dots and realize that Teresa's vision of me at a sacred temple had indeed manifested, just as she predicted. Everything I thought I knew about myself changed dramatically from that moment on — from the way I perceived life in general to the way I viewed religion and faith. Like a rock face that slowly starts to erode, one pebble falls, then another, and soon there are boulders sliding into oblivion. My dreams were filled with shadows, my waking life constantly shifting, and through it all a sense of helplessness. It was all coming undone.

My relationship with Dave ended pretty much on schedule. I sat with him in a small café on September 9, 2001 — two days before the events that would change the world forever — as he told me in a very pragmatic way that he wanted out of the relationship. I tried to handle the news as best I could, but inevitably crumbled. It was all I could do to complete the physical act of separation, find a new place to live, and fall into the office of a good therapist for the next six months. And still the words of the psychic kept repeating in my head "You will suffer more than you've ever imagined. But after the pain come new revelations."

You may be wondering at this point what all of this has to do with the book you are holding in your hands. The answer is 'everything.' If there's one thing I've learned through all of this, it's that there can be no single event in one's life that can be set aside from all of the others, no event so distinct that it can be viewed without consideration of the whole. Everything counts. There are no coincidences. Life is indeed a journey. My decision to write A Voice in the Forest was more than the sum of pen to paper — it was an agreement made across the boundaries of life and death — a leap of faith into a void. And there was no way I could have anticipated the tsunami-like effects it would cause in every area of my life. For starters, Alex did not remain silent following the final pages of A Voice in the Forest. Although less frequent, the communications do continue up to the present. Because Alex is once again incarnate (the extraordinary details of which have been chronicled in this expanded edition), the manner in which he communicates is slightly more complex than before. In addition, given the many personal challenges that I have faced over the past few years, maintaining a sense of connection to Alex has not always been a pleasant experience. When he does come through, perhaps because his connection with us has been so tenuous, he can be very aggressive. I sense that this is due to the fact that there is so little time to communicate with us, and that the dynamics of these sessions are constantly shifting. Sometimes the intensity of his messages borders on confrontation. It is as if he is drawing lines in the sand and daring us to cross them. Sometimes I perceive him as a fish out of water — gasping for air — a man so desperate to push just one message through the void that separates us that there is little room for protocol. This does not mean, however, that he is beyond compassion. His love of the Craft and the goddess still prevails and he frequently mentions friends and family by name and shows genuine concern for their welfare. But there is also a sense of urgency to his communications.

There is little time for chatter, he seems to be saying. There is too much work still to be done.

If I could sum up what seems to be Alex's present state of mind (if such a term can even apply, given the nature of our interaction with him), I would say he is disillusioned over the current state of the Craft. Although the dual themes of preserving the Craft for the future and finding the true heart of the goddess still pervade his communications, there is more of an edge now — a kind of frantic concern about our communal state of affairs. Because I sense Alex so acutely, this has caused me to re-think much of what I believe to be true about the Craft today. I see Alex as inhabiting a world of Magick and Mystery — a world where anything is possible — a world in which death is not an ending, but a beginning, in which each day brings a new opportunity to learn and grow. The spiritual evolution of our souls is a complex business and takes many lifetimes to accomplish. The canvas that we paint is much broader than this moment in time.

When I say that I sense Alex's disillusionment with the current state of the Craft, I don't intend to negate the great progress that all of us have made over the years in making our religion more palatable to the general public. However, I do suggest that in the process we may have lost something important — our own unique identity, our unapologetic love of the occult — in short, the dark beating heart of the Craft itself — something that defies gentle explanation. In an age where ritual and magick are easily tamed by politics and potlucks, it is often difficult to measure what we have gained against what we have lost.

I never had the pleasure of knowing Alex Sanders in his lifetime, but I imagine he was a man who lived it without boundaries, a man who broke all of the rules. When I visualize him, it is not the young coffee table book Alex that I see, but a man who dedicated his entire life to the Craft, a man whose mortal days ended well outside of the spotlight.

A friend of Alex's recently described to me how, in his final months, he would take a bus to and from the hospital where he was being treated for cancer, the place where he would eventually die. On his final journey there he carried a small suitcase with a few of his personal belongings. This suitcase and its contents have since come into the possession of Graham King, the curator of the Witchcraft Museum in Boscastle, England. Although not part of the excellent permanent exhibit, Graham was kind enough to permit my friends Asha and Finbar a glimpse of the contents. Asha's tearful recollection of the mundane items it contained — a pair of slippers, a belt, a simple kitchen knife (reminiscent of Aleister Crowley's pocket knife which served as an athame in his final, impoverished days) — have helped me to understand not only the inevitable human frailty of Alex Sanders (and by extension, my own), but also his tremendous spiritual accomplishments. He attained over many lifetimes a level of adeptness that is staggering to contemplate. In the pages of new material included in this second edition, you will have read of how Alex returned twice to the Lammas woods described in the first encounter in 1998 and of how these communications continue even though he is now physically reincarnated in the body of a small boy.

Recently I spent an afternoon at the Metropolitan Museum of Art in New York City, wandering the galleries of classic European paintings. I started to see art in a new way on that visit, and I think the analogy will fit well as a summation of how my perception of just about everything has changed since writing this book.

Gazing at one of these grand paintings, I first beheld the obvious — a work of art in totality. It all appears to be there — a hand emerging gracefully from a ruffled cuff, the sheen of satin dresses, a vase of flowers forever blooming on a dining table, a path leading into the dark woods. But what I didn't see was the creation of the painting itself, the years of work put into the canvas, the life of the artist behind the painting. What was the artist's day like when they painted those trees? Were they happy or sad when the flowers fell from their brush onto the canvas' vase? What pain, what pleasure did they feel when each stroke of the brush was made? In looking at the broader canvas, it is possible to see both the painter and the painting — a life constantly in the act of creation and creating, one made up of millions of delicate brush strokes, defined and redefined moment to moment by an ever-expanding vision — a vision that is perpetually changing as we are all changing. First we are a sky at dusk — fading to dark with maybe just a hint of violet light   then we are a bright summer morning with a riot of flowers around us. And it all matters. It is all an integral part of the whole package. But in the end, the artist is gone and the painting alone remains. The painting becomes the soul of the artist.

Alex Sanders, always an innovator, once again defies the rules. He still stands somewhere with a brush in his hands, never content that the painting is done. And the rest of us must paint like madmen while we can

Jimahl DiFiosa

still make a difference.

Jimahl DiFiosa

UNEDITED CHANNELING SESSIONS

A Voice in the Forest

Jimahl DiFiosa

In the first edition of A Voice in the Forest, some of the more dramatic communication with Alex Sanders occurred during the automatic writing sessions. I edited the text of these communications before publication for several reasons. I knew the channeled messages were controversial at best and I was overly concerned about how they would be perceived. I tried to set my ego aside and complete the task that Alex had given to me, and yet I was also genuinely concerned about public ridicule. And lastly, some of the dialogue with Alex (particularly in the third session) seemed to take on almost apocalyptic tones, which frightened me.
Included below is the full unedited text of these channeling sessions.

SESSION ONE

I am Alex Sanders King of the Witches. It has been a long time since I wrote, spoke, moved about in the physical world. Many of you have no doubt forgotten me. Some have not. I would hope that you are in remembrance of me. But I was a man and men die all the time. It is dark here. There is no light. A kind of purgatory I suppose if you think of the after-life as a waiting room of sorts. I could have reincarnated long ago, but I chose to remain earthbound. So I am caught be-tween the worlds. I drift like smoke about you. I inhabit your rooms, your sacred spaces. My spirit goes to the circles where I am welcome. I observe. I watch. I try to teach but it is difficult unless those incarnate are receptive. For who can listen to the words of a spirit, not a man who can stand up and be counted as one to hear, but a spirit of a man once known as King of the Witches. Even now there is rancor among you. There is division. There is doubt that I can exist in this way and in this time. But the irony is that this is the natural order of things. I can do what I wish. I have attained that power in many past lives. I am what I say I am, King of the Witches, and abeyance is due me, if not for any other reason but that I am the forefather of who you are. And as I now am so you will be and your children's children shall look after you as you look after me. And so the Craft goes on — it never dies. It never stops. It can't — you must see to that. I could care less if you use my name 100 years from now. But the goddess must have her due worship. I won't wear you out, I promise. Just relax and let me speak. It is interesting seeing how this computer works. I should have liked that. Now where were we? I am Alex Sanders, of that there is no doubt. You can take that to the bank, as they say. I want to talk about the goddess. And the Craft of the goddess — that which is and always has been and that which will continue for ages to come. I want to tell you about power, personal power, fulfillment of your every wish. I want to teach you what I could not teach you in my lifetime. I want to show you the way of all true magick. I want to continue. You will tell me if you need me to stop. There is a great circle of life and of being that encompasses all humanity. I can see it from here. We are connected on every level. You often make the mistake in perception to think that your lives begin and end at the end of your own existence. Imagine yourself as the center piece of a great wheel. You seem complete in yourself. You can turn and move in any direction. You are a circle and your hands, the tips of your fingers, the toes on your feet all touch the perimeter of the circle. But there is so much more. I will leave you now. We'll start again another time. Be in peace and goddess rest.

SESSION TWO

I am Alex Sanders, King of the Witches. I come to you from across the eons. I watch the fire of the sun illuminate a fertile land. I see how difficult it is for those who follow the old ways to see the path that will lead them forward, to recognize the dangers that lay before them. I understand how hard it is for those who love the goddess to keep a clear mind and unfettered will so that they can be about her business without interference from those who would declaim her virtues and deny even the most basic rights to those who follow her. This is a strange new world. I find myself inside it as an archetype. I am out of my element. Around me there are faces I do not know and when I seek for those who knew me as a man, there is only silence. There is no reply to my inquiry. I am alone and this is a very dry place for me. I will move on soon as I do not see the need for me to remain earthbound much longer. How quickly they turned to the memory of me but, once the time moves by and they forget, then the memory of me fades quickly like a flower. I am forgotten of many, no longer the King of the Witches, and this causes me much consternation. I see that there is a thread, a river of red life that still flows and it is to this river I am drawn like a moth to the fire. And when I see that there is a circle of elders still following the path I made, I am glad. My spirit rejoices. I understand how important it was to wait until I move on. I see that this has not been in vain. You ask me what I would have you do — I would have you tell the others that magick is real. Witchcraft is real. I devoted my life to it. I saw the age of the goddess dawn over mankind. I came to the Craft in a time when speaking her name was dangerous. I came to her when the dark of the moon was the only time we could worship her for fear of discovery, when the living room became the temple of Isis and the basement, dark and secret, became the place for our library. How we hungered for our freedom then, how we dreamed of a time when we might utter the secret name of the goddess in public without consequence. All of this has come about in a short period of time and even now the cult of the goddess grows. It grows from the dead wood of Christianity, for there are those who see the mother of god as the creatress [sic] and wonder aloud why she has been allowed to squander her power in the shadow of a sacrificial son. I see that she is once again in the forefront of a religion that will continue to progress as the years ahead un¬fold and this is a sign that the way of the goddess will become more palatable to those who seek her. I see that the ways of magick are no longer hidden and you may find the secrets of the ages on any bookshelf in any store. They are so accessible that the reverse danger is evident — that there is a tendency to take all things for granted, to see them as common things that have no weight. This is a trap of the mind and must be avoided. The mysteries of the goddess are stronger and deeper than time. They defy time. And I can see that now more than ever they become visible to anyone who looks with their eyes. As a path in the forest they beckon, and the true seeker has no alternative but to follow. These are amazing times and the keepers of the mysteries must be aware of how critical it is to keep true to the path and to make the way smooth for those who will follow their footsteps. More than ever before man looks for an answer to questions asked for thousands of years.

The secrets of space are open to us. The secrets of the earth are open to us. The secrets of the universe are open to us. How then can any true seeker of the Craft be denied? How then can any true witch, or one that calls themselves a hidden child of the goddess, say there is no magick? For magick is in the word, the spoken word. Magick is in the breath of every child and in the love of the mother for the child — how then can we be sad? How then can we be dismal? Wake up the heart that slumbers and look to the dawn of a new day for it is a glorious dawn.

I come to you now as a teacher and entrust you with these words. As fantastic as it seems to you, you must be brave enough to pass them on to any who will listen. You must allow me the opportunity to speak once more before all is changed — before the end of the eon. For there has never been a better time to look at the facts as they are. I devoted my life to the goddess, but as a man I made many mistakes. That is the mortal way and unavoidable to the most ingenious of us. I pissed people off, to say it bluntly. I turned them against me, particularly at the end when there was no place for me to go but down and it seemed as if they all waited for it outside my door. Like wolves they waited and when the king was dead they wailed like children. How sad I am that I did not have more time, or the knowledge that alluded me all those years that I lusted after like golden flesh. I hungered for a touch of the goddess and she came to me again and again and still I wanted more. I deserved it, I told myself. She owed it to me. The goddess, as we see her, is so small. She is just a piece of our mortal fancies and we envision her in manageable portions. Like a piece of meat upon our plates, we cut her up and examine her and when we swallow we want to be certain we don't choke ourselves with her. So she becomes small and insignificant. We dress her and adorn her with memories of past lives and we awaken within ourselves the threads of memory that allow us to see her in a way that does not consume us. But when we awaken any aspect of the true goddess, we awaken the great beast of the goddess that has no safety valve attached. We can't deflate her by pulling a cork.

She is big, beyond any reasoning — beyond any imagining — and a true invocation of the goddess takes one into the abyss. We must be prepared to experience all of her — not just the parts of her that we are comfortable with. She is a beautiful goddess — but she is all that is and was and will be. The earth is the body of the goddess and the earth moves and shakes and shudders beneath us. The earth can heal and it also destroys — it swallows us whole without apology and begs for more. So the primordial goddess is more than we can envision and the words of a priest of the goddess must be chosen carefully for this reason. I honor her. I adore her. And there is no reason for me not to endorse her to you, for the way of the goddess is the path of truth.

Go to her then and be absorbed by her — even when she breaks you down you will profit in the end. There are many who profess to know her and who speak the way of magick. Perhaps they read the books and memorize what it is that they feel they should know — but they do not know her. Their lives are devoid of her. They are limited by fears that manage their lives. This fear dictates what they will never become and when it comes time for them to exercise will over matter they cannot do so. They are the slave to matter. Their will is undeveloped, and that is a danger to them.

Know then that many are called but few are chosen. Even among your own you can see those that have come to the goddess untruthfully. They stand on ground that is not solid. Even among your own you must recognize those who are the old souls who have walked this path before. Magick then is serious business. You cannot fool with it without consequence. Mind my words lest you destroy yourself with your own pride. That is the first lesson I would leave you. Be true to your Craft and do not give your word lightly. You must be prepared to back up your word with your life and the goddess may very well demand such allegiance one day. Why then have I come now to speak this way through you. The answer is simple — you are willing to allow me to move through you. I will use you by your own invitation to say what I will say. And then I will walk away. You ask what it is I want to say and I shall reveal it to you in time. It has been a long while since I had a voice. I must pace myself, and for your safety, I will proceed with caution.

THIRD SESSION

You sense me near but are unable to touch, to communicate with me, and this frustrates you greatly. I am equally frustrated because I cannot speak to you the way in which you desire. I cannot see you in the way in which you ask me to see you. There are shadows between this world and the next and except in a consecrated circle there is much interference. I hear you. I sense you. But it is difficult for me to speak in return, to touch and to answer your many questions. The tie that binds us together is the tie of love for each other. Although I do not know you, I see the goddess in you and I respond to her. The tie of love that binds us is the love of the Craft that you show forth and I respond to it as I must. I am Alex Sanders. I am he who you call your forefather. It is good that you are where you are at this point in time for there are many who profess to know the gods and yet so few do. You vanquish over fallen idols and see that the city of the gods is laid ruin by those who have broken her down. They have dissected her and taken the heart of her to offer to the gods of high commerce, of technology, of civilization. And still the barbaric heart of man shows his true face, for there is never peace in the world. The fighting and the shouting, the civil disobedience all will continue for the way of this civilization is ruin and death. The reason for my presence is clear only to me, for it is a path that I have chosen. How long will I remain here? You say there are many who care to listen but in reality there are few who care anymore. There are greater teachers than I to come. I have made a small mark on the face of the cult of the goddess. I would do more if I could. My time is up and I must go soon into the void, as you would see it. I pass over soon into the heart of the goddess and from there await rebirth. I call you now to service and you respond. You rise to the challenge and bravely put forth what I tell you onto the written page. Some will read and understand and the words will be like fodder for their fires and others will read and not understand — it doesn't matter. It doesn't. For all things come to nothing in the end if the heart is not pure. The season of change is upon us, for there is change beyond knowing on the horizon.

The children of the goddess must unite in their efforts, for never again the burning times. I cannot see beyond, but I can tell you that even now the astral grows crowded with weary travelers that seek the light of the circle. I sense that many are not worthy and yet the living grow weary. Be strong in purpose and pure in heart. As long as a circle is cast, as long as the name of the goddess is invoked, she will manifest and grow fat with worship. I cannot say more than that.

Never quit.

Never stop, for the effort alone carries you forward. Believe in yourself. Believe in the power of your own commitment.

Jimahl DiFiosa

ALEX SANDERS ON ADEPTNESS AND REENCARNATION

AN INTERVIEW WITH ALEX SANDERS, 26TH NOVEMBER, 1974 BY LORIEL

A Voice in the Forest

Jimahl DiFiosa

NOTE: *I was talking with Alex at Chantry Cottage, Bexhill, Sussex, where he was living at the time, the home of 'BB'. We were doing some work together and the questions relate to a part of that. Alex's answers were recorded on a tape of poor quality and transcribed later. Some bits were unintelligible due to noise of various kinds: people in the house, glasses clinking, people talking in background. The tape was switched on halfway through and some of the questions and answers refer to things that had been discussed earlier, before the tape was turned on. The transcript is verbatim, "ums," "ahs" and all, and I've added some notes where I think it might clarify what was going on. My own notes shall be in italics within parentheses. [Multiple question marks within indicate unintelligible responses. Ed.]*

LORIEL: How would you describe your position within the occult hierarchies, not only in this country, but in the world?

ALEX: I can only say from the point of view of witchcraft and ceremonial magick that I'm probably one of the only real practitioners in existence, and I base this on this reason — on this fact — that the Golden Dawn is supposed to be the leading occult order in this century, and when people like Francis King have wanted to illustrate their books with Golden Dawn trappings, photographs of Golden Dawn circles and temples, they ask me to set them up, even though he's supposed to be in contact with various groups of the Order.

LORIEL: They still exist, do they?

ALEX: They're still in existence and (??) supposed to be in touch with lots of things — not one of them is capable of setting up the Golden Dawn rituals or temple. I'm the only one so capable, to have it photographed, set it up.

LORIEL: When I was reading that book yesterday by John Symonds, he said that Crowley had gone with one of his women, I forget which, to the Far East, and he went to see Alan Bennett, who was by then a bhikku (Buddhist monk), and he opened the door and he saw, to his amazement, that Bennett was hovering about four feet off the floor —

ALEX: I don't believe it — that's just Crowley.

LORIEL: But Symonds does say that —

ALEX: I don't believe it. He (Crowley) did a send up. He (Alan Bennett) is now buried in Golders Green (N. London suburb) or somewhere like that, in London (??)...

LORIEL: But Symonds did say that he'd chosen the higher life of the spirit, meaning the Buddhist meditations, rather than the play-acting, almost, of the Golden Dawn. I mean, do you think that's what it had become?

ALEX: I think the Golden Dawn had too much Masonry mixed up in what it was doing, although it did have some good stuff. I find a lot of it incredibly childish, though. A lot of its people had high academic backgrounds and lots of money or (??) do better — my education had practically finished when I was 13 and a half... Although I couldn't speak languages, I could penetrate the depths of a ritual, and portray it, I feel, in a much more honest way, and a much more dramatic way. That's why I get criticized, because the drama of what I do is very sensational. What people don't realize is the spirit that's coming through, they only recognise the physical impact of it. (??) This is why I've instilled fear into a lot of people with public appearances.

LORIEL: I'm going to come back to this, actually, right at the end.

ALEX: (Continued from tape.) ... But I get decried for that kind of thing.

LORIEL: When Crowley was initiated into the Golden Dawn, he was quite disappointed, wasn't he? They took him aside with great ceremony and gave him a list of Hebrew letters.

ALEX: Yes, well I think he'd only just packed it into a few words, and he was making fun. Making fun in an annoying sort of way, because if anyone said to me as far as ceremonial magick — put me into an occult order — and said this is our secret, and it's based on the 22 letters of the Hebrew alphabet — and the letters of the alphabet are symbols, and the symbols are numbers, and the numbers are the primitive hieroglyphics, and upon this is based the whole of the cosmic universe.... You know, he could have given a bit more detail than that — then said "now we come to the forces behind the principles, now we come to the principles themselves, now we come to the elements, now we come to the emanations of the elements, now we come to the beginnings of creation." He was quite right when he said that's all they gave to him — that's all they did, and at the end of everything, if I teach anybody whatever occult system, Western, Eastern or even ancient Egyptian, all I can do is relate it to the Tree of Life, which is the finest composite glyph in the whole of the world.

LORIEL: I was really coming to the (Golden Dawn's) stages of occult development, Crowley's development progressed through very definite stages, didn't it? From novice... (Here I was wanting to get to Alex's own development, which was in GD terms most unorthodox, but the discussion got sidetracked as follows:)

ALEX: Yes, but those grades — don't be led astray by the names of the grades either — they're very Masonic, the de-grees of squares are very Masonic, and they're only a sliding scale for that particular Order. You know, in the Wicca we have exactly the same thing, except that it's scaled to three. Now that three can be fitted onto the Tree of Life. The first degree is Hod, Netzach, including Yesod, to Malkuth. The second degree includes Geburah, Tiphareth, Yesod, Hod, Netzach and Malkuth. And then the third degree includes the whole supernal, and it lifts man to Godhead and brings Godhead down to man. It's like Jacob and the angels going up and down the ladder....

LORIEL: What I was going to ask, really, was when one of the adepts of the Golden Dawn had reached Adeptus Exemptus, which was the last stage of the second order, they used to symbolically "cross the Abyss..."

ALEX: Yes.

LORIEL: ... which was this tremendous killing of the 'ego,' as far as I understand it —

ALEX: Yes, and they became more egotistical afterwards. More concerned with what 'I' am going to do. They became all powerful and there was only 'I' in existence and nobody else.

LORIEL: Those last three grades of Magister Templi, Magus and Ipsissimus... now as far as I've always understood it and I'm probably quite wrong... but someone who had reached the grade of Ipsissiumus was right at the top of the magickal tree, as far as he could go without being merged into the Light — the emanations... now when you say that the three grades of witchcraft are comparable to that, do you mean to say that someone who is a third grade witch is comparable to... (My point was going to be that I did not believe that a third grade witch could be comparable to Ipsissimus.)

ALEX: Yes, is Adeptus.

LORIEL: ...comparable in stature to... (Here we were clearly at cross purposes.)

ALEX: Yes, I had to have a title given to me, granted to me, whether I felt I was capable of receiving it or not — the title literally of the Grand Master of All the Witches... was the greatest compliment to my work that I'd done, but they chose me for that degree. They saw the emanation, I didn't. I still don't, actually. And I always hate the fact I've been stuck with it... And yet my horoscope — working out of my horoscope — was done anonymously

(??), and the two people who did it still didn't know, and still don't know to this day, whose hand or whose horoscope they did. And they said this man has the powers of a king, and must be a ruler of some kind. So what was given to me was either destined or decreed for me...

LORIEL: What I was interested in doing, having said all that, was through your life, tracing the various stages of development — is that the right word, do you think? (We had
been discussing me writing a book about Alex's life.)

ALEX: Yes, but I haven't taken it like this.

LORIEL: I know you haven't —

ALEX: — the steps along (???), because I've been married three times, and many love affairs in between. And according to the love that you're giving out, and according to the surroundings and the people, and the environment, so your approach to a system differs. And many of the things that I've done wouldn't be acceptable to the adepts. Like the adepts laugh at me when I say an angel told me to go and get a job in the library (John Rylands Library, Manchester) and to go and get the Key of Solomon, to get Abramelin, and I went and got the job, and they say to me, didn't you realize you could go to Watkins (an occult bookshop in Cecil Court, London) and buy it? But I got it the real way, you see, I didn't go to a shop and buy a book. I was told where it was. I underwent a lot of privitation [sic] to get that. I took the humblest job, in a place where I knew as much about Egyptology as the governor and the people who were in charge of the ancient Egyptian section.

LORIEL: So in fact, your development has been totally unorthodox, you know, in their terms, but natural in another way?

ALEX: Yes.

LORIEL (This from BB.): Wouldn't it be true to say that it has been an interior development, rather than a seeking for external —

ALEX: Yes, I was on the outside without belonging in orders. I didn't belong to any order, until... if you discount churches, discount Christian religion — I didn't belong to any Orders such as Knights Templars, Order of St Michael, St George — sixteen of them, until 1968.

LORIEL: How did you actually get involved with those orders then? Did people approach you?
(I was thinking of a time at the flat in Notting Hill, London, when I'd opened the basement door to an elderly gentleman who was coming down the steps with a gift for Alex, a brown paper bag of oranges. He said to me, "Please tell Alex the Prince is here." Alex told me later that the visitor was Prince Petros Paleologos, Grand Master of the Ordine Della Luna in Constantinople, one of the chivalric orders to which Alex refers here.)

ALEX: Because of my secret works of charity. They caught up with me. I was presented for good works, good Christian works, even though they knew who I was. I belong to the real Knights Templars, not the pseudo-magickal Knights Templars ... (??) time of Constantine the Great, and before.

LORIEL: This point I've noted about past lives... I think that's probably interesting enough to give a complete discussion on its own to, don't you?

ALEX: Yes, I won't be able to give you too much detail — only brief descriptions of what I felt. I can go back to, well I think, Norse times, when I know the people of the tribe worshipped a piece of wood and put furs and things around it. And that I was a girl, and that girls were there for fucking and for nothing else. And that there was a man who used to take me along to — well it must have been his home or my home — because I'd just get dragged down and fucked and that was the end of me... I'd to get food.... Then I was told that I hadn't got to go down near the river because the man of the water would get me. And it was all silver and he was all glittering with scales.... And the spirit of the water would come out and make me pregnant, would give me a baby. It would be half fish and half human, and I went down there and he swam across the water and he got me. Now, in this life, I know that he belonged to another tribe of water dwellers, and when the forest dwellers (??) half fish, and he actually did make me pregnant, and I went back home and I remember dying in childbirth, with blood all over me and hearing them say that she wouldn't last. And uncovering the — I think it was an oak stump — it's got some bark in front like a face, and uncovering me, and the whole place was stinking and full of smoke — and that's what this (Here he pointed at a wood fire.) reminds me of (??)... And the next time I remember I was swimming in water and I was (??), and I was literally a pearl fisherman, not in this part of the world. I have no feeling for the Orient. The Orient is just distant from me, and Chinese things — Japanese things — don't really appeal to me, even though I've got a Chinese spirit. And literally going down to catch — well not to catch oysters, but to get them, to dig them up — and my lungs bursting, through going down too many times, and I was only young, only 13 or 14....

I remember another life in Bangkok, in the temple on the hill — I believe it still exists — in the White Temple. Probably about the 7th century AD. When I was taken out to be initiated I was still a little boy, probably 5 or 6 years old, being put into a boat with a lot of other boys and three men rowing, and watching — going across this ornamental lake which appeared to be very big, to a great big dome, like a (cluster?) of domes, being taken in through great bronze doors (??) and knowing that my brothers and sisters and parents, and older brothers and sisters were all on the banks, and knowing that I'd become part of the sacred mystery. And being in there and we were taught how to do the snake dance there, and how to wear (??)... and suddenly the doors and galleries were crowded with priests watching and guarding, and suddenly the doors seemed to come straight down and these people came in and — we were literally in rows along the floor, still in position, so well trained that I wouldn't even move and carrying on to the next position and watching this man come across me with a knife, and just slicing me right the way through, and watching all this bubble out — just burst out. And that was another life gone.... Another time again — it all seems to be with water — swimming, and swimming away from somebody, and wearing red and blue clothes, woven clothes, of cotton, probably somewhere in Egypt, I think. And swimming across this marshy stream, and this other young man, could be 22, 23 years old, throwing a great big stone and it hitting me on the head, and going down, and feeling the water gush into my mouth, and not being able to swallow it ... and not being able to swallow it ... and swallowing and swallowing until I just felt myself go, just like a (??).... The Egyptian lives — I prefer not to go into just at this moment, because when we start to work with it, I'll try to go back and let you speak to the actual beings, and then you'll get an accurate account.... (Tape is imperfect and inaudible at this point.)

LORIEL: I was going to ask you about the creation of Michael ... out of the June Johns account, you know, I grasped the two major things ....

ALEX: To tell you about Michael in detail and exactly I'd have to have the Book of the Dead. To show you how one arrives at the conclusion of the creation —

LORIEL: — I've got a copy of it.

ALEX: Bring it with you the next time and we'll go into detail about it — I can't describe it ... because the vignettes need description — it would be interesting to point out the vignettes with all the numbers. And even how we use the numbers to bring powers down. And this very real creation (??) — crunchy bars are still up there for him. He still gets his gifts of crunchies.... (Spirit Michael loved 'crunchy' bars, a kind of chocolate bar.) Yes, I will go into detail about my Egyptian initiations.

LORIEL: Personally, I'm fascinated by the Egyptian things....

ALEX: Well, they were Atlanteans really, weren't they?

LORIEL: There must be huge chunks of stuff that no¬body knows about, you know — as the covens built up from say one, to —

ALEX: Yes, to whatever they are. Yes — lots of stuff, because people have not been interested in the detail when they've been with me, they've been interested in me rather than what I do, and the sensational side of me, the side which makes the impact publicly, the side that's not said "no" to making a record — I've thought of leaving records of my work, and I've chosen the modern media for it, such as making an LP, such as a cabaret, you know a cabaret and mystery play put together ....

(NOTE: Tape ends here.)

Jimahl DiFiosa

◇—
RESPONSES TO A VOICE IN THE FOREST

A Voice in the Forest

Jimahl DiFiosa

Following the publication of A Voice in the Forest, I received many correspondences from around the globe. Many wrote to say how moved they were by the book ("Did you know what a blessing your book would be when you wrote it?") or how Alex's message helped guide them through a difficult period of time ("I was about to give up on the Craft after suffering a real crisis of faith. But when I finished reading your book, I decided to go back into active teaching again.") Some letters were not so warm and fuzzy — one reader seemed genuinely confused as to why Alex would choose to communicate with an 'American witch over a British witch.' But the most wonderful letters came from Alex's closest friends. The following letter is being published here for the first time — and I share it to highlight the serendipitous inclusion of the Alex Sanders interview, above. JdF

Dear Jimahl,
Well here it is, finally. Copied from my original transcript of twenty-six years ago! Working back through it, Alex was powerfully present for me. I could hear his voice, and his gestures and intonations came back to me. The original tape is still around somewhere, I think, and there may be others. I don't know what use this will be to you. I hope at least it will be interesting. When I first got in touch with you, to ask where I could buy your book, I didn't ever envisage that there would be any further communication between us, but I think it was when you said you felt Alex would have wanted me to have a copy — and then when I read it — that it occurred to me that perhaps Alex, if he can still affect our destinies from beyond death, had also wanted you to have these memories that I have of him. So let me know if you find this of any value, and I'll try to look out for some more stuff. Also, if you ever visit this country, or Europe, please do let me know and I would like to take you round some of the places

where Alex lived
and worked, especially here in Sussex.

With all good wishes, Blessed Be,
Loriel

Printed in Great Britain
by Amazon